THE LEARNING ENVIRONMENT:
An
Instructional Strategy

THE LEARNING ENVIRONMENT: An Instructional Strategy

Catherine E. Loughlin   Joseph H. Suina
The University of New Mexico

Teachers College, Columbia University
New York and London
1982

Published by Teachers College Press, 1234 Amsterdam Avenue,
New York, N.Y. 10027

Library of Congress Cataloging in Publication Data

Loughlin, Catherine E., 1927–
The learning environment.

Bibliography: p.
Includes index.
1.   School environment   2.   Classroom management.
I.   Suina, Joseph H.   II.   Title.
LC210.L68   371.1'02   81-23353
                                     AACR2

ISBN 0-8077-2714-8

Illustrations by
Dave Black
Manufactured in the United States of America
87   86   85   84   83   82   1   2   3   4   5   6

Dedicated to
Lorraine Suina and Eleanor Warren
Mavis Martin and Lucy Laughlin

CONTENTS

SECTION II: PROVISIONING FOR LEARNING

FOREWORD

The prominent literature of education today, especially the new genre associated with "effective schools," has a defensive character; it tends to support a narrow view of schools and their possibilities with achievement as measured by outcomes on a range of standardized tests characterized as the overarching mission of schools. Formula driven, the roles of teachers, principals, and students are circumscribed by precise, rather confining definitions. While there is a good deal of attention in this literature to the need for high expectations, "effective schools" are described for the most part as minimalist settings. It is not an inspiring literature. It doesn't challenge individuals in schools to be thoughtful, creative in their uses of materials and settings, to view classrooms and schools as educative morally and aesthetically as well as academically, as places where fragile human relationships are cemented, where language learning and communication have meaning beyond simple constructs, where a wide variety of community connections and continuities are affirmed as well as challenged, where divergence of thought and action are valued and the present lives of children acknowledged and respected. *The Learning Environment,* by Joseph Suina and Catherine Loughlin is qualitatively different and for that reason is particularly attractive to me and others with whom I work.

The Learning Environment is about the use of space writ large; active rather than passive metaphors dominate its pages. It captures much of what John Dewey implied when he encouraged teachers to be "students of teaching," persons who developed and maintained a reflective capacity, becoming in the process clear about their intentions and able to make independent judgments about their classrooms. Suina and Loughlin quickly dismiss the architecture, textbooks, size of tables or chairs, or the number of chalkboards and bulletin boards as critical determiners of the environment. They focus their attention instead on teacher thought and decision making. They tend to ask in response to a teacher's concern about children's lack of independence, for example, what have you done to encourage independence? Do children know where the materials they need are stored? How are they organized? Are the materials easily accessible? In response to a concern about children's lack of interest in science or reading they might ask: What kinds of materials do you use? How varied are they? Where are they placed in the classroom? How are they displayed? What else is near them? How visible are they from different parts of the room? Where does science fit in the daily schedule?

Most of us know that when we observe an object carefully from a different perspective, we often see it differently, gaining in the process fresh understanding. We know also from our experience that our interests, moods, openness to new ideas, and willingness to engage particular materials are often influenced by environmental factors. Why then are we so encumbered, as Suina and Loughlin suggest, by "habitual ways of seeing and thinking about classrooms" that we fail to see the myriad alternative possibilities? Shaking that encumbrance is a major object of this book and it accomplishes that end by integrating in a consonant manner a progressive philosophical position about teaching and learning with concrete, real classroom examples about "arranging the environment." To assist teachers who wish to begin an examination of their classroom environments, the authors provide large numbers of thought-provoking illustrations as well as several interesting and helpful methods for teachers to use in "checking their environment" and relating the environment to learning and behavioral concerns.

I began this foreword by commenting negatively about much of the contemporary literature of education. *The Learning Environment* is an important contrast; it helps reaffirm in a practical, understandable manner the critical importance of the teacher and the professionalism inherent in the teacher's role. It places before us a vision of what is possible for children and their learning when teacher intelligence is engaged and respected.

I have appreciated my interactions with the authors over a number of years as they have formulated their ideas and tested them with teachers in large numbers of classrooms. I am pleased that they have brought their efforts together in this wonderful book.

Vito Perrone
University of North Dakota
Grand Forks, North Dakota

PREFACE

The arrangement of the environment significantly influences those who occupy it, as has long been recognized by professionals in fields other than education. Every year department store owners, museum curators, optometrists, and countless managers of public and private organizations spend millions of dollars on environments that are designed to produce some desired attitude or behavior on the part of their occupants. Schools and classrooms can benefit from the same careful attention to environment, yet current notions about effective physical environments for classrooms seem to begin and end with the architectural design and basic furnishings. The essential space and necessary number of desks, chairs, books, and shelves are carefully provided. After that, most of the attention given the environment focuses on making and maintaining an interesting and pleasant setting for work.

Until recently, arrangement of the classroom environment has not been widely appreciated as a tool to support the learning process. The literature and teacher training specifically designed to examine the use of the environment in sound teaching practice have been limited to specialized fields of education such as Montessori and other early childhood programs. Since few other teachers have been helped to appreciate the influence of environmental organization, learning environments tend to be arranged in uninformed ways. However, classroom environment is much more than a place to house books, desks, and materials. Carefully and knowingly arranged, the environment adds a significant dimension to a student's educational experience by engaging interest, offering information, stimulating the use of skills, communicating limits and expectations, facilitating learning activities, promoting self-direction, and through these effects supporting and strengthening the desire to learn.

This book offers both a conceptual framework and practical guidance for arranging the learning environment. It will give classroom teachers and future teachers in elementary and early childhood settings a better understanding of the effects of the teacher-arranged environment in which they spend their days with children. Through its text and illustrations, it presents practical information and procedures for making the learning environment supportive. Examples and drawings of environmental arrangements from real classrooms and step-by-step environmental assessment activities will help teachers examine their own learning environments and their effects on classroom behaviors and events. Principals, teacher supervisors, and other school personnel who assist and evaluate teaching will also benefit from viewing the learning environment as an instructional strategy, as shown and described in this book.

We wish to thank all the teachers who invited us into their classrooms and centers to see the learning environment at work, to observe children responding to environmental messages, to sketch and photograph environmental arrangements, and to think together about effective environments. We hope that, as they recognize their own learning environments in these pages, they will remember those visits with pleasure, as we do.

THE LEARNING ENVIRONMENT:
An
Instructional Strategy

CHAPTER 1

THE LEARNING ENVIRONMENT
A Conceptual View

For many years the school architect was considered the creator of the learning environment while the teacher was seen as housekeeper, arranging, provisioning, and decorating. Teachers considered the learning environment as a kind of scenery for teaching and learning, a pleasant yet inert background for classroom life.

However, there is another way of looking at the learning environment and the teacher's role in creating it within an architectural facility. This view recognizes the teacher-arranged environment as an active and pervasive influence on the lives of children and teachers throughout the school day. In the processes of teaching and learning, the physical environment arranged by the teacher has two functions. It provides the setting for learning and at the same time acts as a participant in teaching and learning.

The Architectural Facility

The physical learning environment has two major elements, the architectural facility and the arranged environment. These two interact to strengthen or limit the environment's contributions to children's learning. Each is essential and each influences children's behavior and learning, but the architectural facility and arranged environment have different functions and characteristics.[1]

The architectural facility provides the setting for all the interactions among people and materials that will occur in the learning process. It

[1]*Catherine E. Loughlin, "Understanding the Learning Environment,"* Elementary School Journal 78 (1977): 125–31.

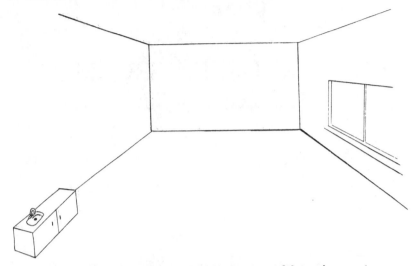

Architectural facilities establish basic spaces of the environment.

establishes the basic space of the environment and organizes access to external spaces and resources. The architectural facility determines basic conditions of light, sound, temperature, and intrusion or separation between groups of people. It provides qualities like color, texture, level, and softness or hardness to the spaces that can be arranged for children's learning.

Today's school facilities tend to offer flexibility in space divisions and in access to indoor and outdoor areas for learning. Some offer considerable variety in the shapes, textures, levels, and sizes of spaces designed for learning. Contemporary school architects consult carefully with educators, community, and students to gain insights for effective design. Whenever possible, facility designers and curriculum planners work together to develop plans for the program and activities of the school's curriculum and for its architecture.[2]

Most architectural facilities are designed to meet school-wide purposes and needs, although there are sometimes special facilities designed for smaller units. Creative architectural designs for clusters or single classrooms depart from enclosed, rectangular, hard-edged, straight-row visions of the learning environment. Many offer soft and hard, curved and angled, smooth and textured, many-leveled surroundings, often flowing between indoor and outdoor spaces without barriers. Sometimes

[2]*Anthony S. Jones, "A New Breed of Learning Environment Consultants,"* in Designing Learning Environments, *ed. Phillip J. Sleeman and D.M. Rockwell (New York: Longman, 1981), pp. 46–48.*

the specialized facility designs include furnishings, many fixed and some movable.[3]

School designs based on studies of current and projected program styles offer settings that are harmonious with those programs. In such facilities the development of the teacher-arranged environment is well supported by the setting, provided the teacher's plans and methods closely resemble the programs that were studied.[4] However, even with the closest possible match between facility and program style, the architectural facility can fulfill only some of the functions of the physical environment for learning; it is not, in itself, the learning environment. This is because architectural facilities are generalized and within the time frame of the school year tend to be static.

Architectural facilities are designed in terms of a generalized prediction of behaviors, activities, functioning levels of students, teaching purposes, and teaching styles associated with the planned curriculum. As the environment is put to use, a variety of teachers, each with a specific group of children, inhabit spaces within the facility. Each teacher has an agenda with its own set of behavior expectations, learning experiences, routines, skills to be practiced, and knowledge to be acquired. For each, the pattern is specific and related to the unique group of learners involved. The development of the arranged environment, so as to fit the specific children and the specific program, will be easier in a setting harmonious with the teacher's agenda than in a setting that conflicts. In even the best of facilities, however, teachers must further develop the generalized environment for specific purposes and groups.

There is considerable variation among architectural facilities in the proportion of fixed and movable features, and in the amount of flexibility offered. Yet within that portion of the facility in which an individual or teaching team works with children, the architectural environment tends to remain basically unchanged through the school year. Free-standing lofts are too heavy to be shifted often, movable walls aren't changed on a weekly basis, and folding partitions are treated like walls even when opened. Although children's competencies, skills, and interests change a good deal in the course of a school year, the architectural facility isn't easily changed to make day-to-day, immediate, short-term adaptations in spatial organization and material distribution patterns. Such adaptations are necessary responses to the continuous change of needs and activities associated with children's growth. The architectural facility

[3]*Anne P. Taylor and George Vlastos,* School Zone: Learning Environments for Children *(New York: Van Nostrand Reinhold, 1975), pp. 58–61.*

[4]*Etta Proshansky and Maxine Wolfe, "The Physical Setting and Open Education," in* Learning Environments, *ed. Thomas G. David and Benjamin D. Wright (Chicago: University of Chicago Press, 1975), pp. 31–48.*

can only provide the settings in which the daily adaptations of the arranged environment occur.

The architectural facility is the beginning of the learning environment, forming the framework within which the teacher establishes the arranged environment. It must be complemented by the continuous work of provisioning and organizing space and materials for learners in response to their growth.

The Arranged Environment

The active and responsive elements of the learning environment are arranged by teachers within the spaces and settings provided by architectural design and construction. The learning environment is more than a building, arrangements of furniture, or collections of interest centers. A conceptual view of the arranged environment is a much larger and at the same time a more basic concept. It rests upon understandings of relationships between physical settings and behavior, between environmental arrangements and learning. Common principles can be derived from this knowledge, and they can be used to establish arranged environments harmonious with program purposes and styles in many different settings. Each environment developed in this way is unique, being responsive to

The active elements of the environment are teacher-arranged.

and appropriate for individual children and teachers. Developed on the basis of environmental principles, the arranged environment can be used as an instructional strategy, complementing and reinforcing other strategies the teacher uses to support children's learning.

Environment as a Tool

The learning environment can be a powerful teaching instrument at the disposal of the teacher, or it can be an undirected and unrecognized influence on the behaviors of both teachers and children. Informed attention to the arranged environment, and the conscious use of it to support program goals, have not been widespread in elementary schools, but understanding environmental influences is important for all teachers, no matter what the age of the students or how formal or informal the programs. Knowledge of the relationships between physical surroundings and actions is a practical tool the teacher can use for many purposes. Teachers can predict behavior in classroom settings. They can teach through the environment and its materials. Many management tasks can be carried out through environmental arrangements so the teacher doesn't have to preside over them. This releases teacher time from management and gives more time for productive interactions with children.[5]

Predicting Behavior

When a teacher understands what events are likely to occur within particular arrangements of materials or space, it is possible to make

[5]*Catherine E. Loughlin, "Arranging the Learning Environment," Insights 11 (1978): 2–5.*

The environment can be a powerful teaching tool.

Low complexity makes adult assistance necessary.

predictions about children's behavior. For instance, provisioning at a high level of complexity usually promotes involvement and a fairly long attention span for pupils, combined with independence from teacher assistance and direction. A low level of complexity brings frequent activity change, physical movement, shorter attention span, and a need for adult direction and assistance.[6] The ability to predict behavior in certain settings means that teachers can arrange settings to promote particular actions.

Environment as Teacher

Teachers can easily arrange and position learning materials so the materials themselves play an active role in the teaching-learning process. Since displaying materials side by side strongly suggests connections between them and the possibility of combining them in some way, combinations of materials can suggest activities.[7] Students are less apt to make connections between widely separated materials or to combine them in learning activities, except with teacher direction. Thus the placement of print references and writing tools in areas traditionally reserved for manipulative materials or natural specimens, is a way to stimulate the use of some basic skills while children use those concrete

[6]*Elizabeth Jones,* Dimensions of Teaching-Learning Environments: Handbook for Teachers *(Pasadena: Pacific Oaks College Bookstore, 1973), p. 12.*

[7]*Sybil Kritchevsky, Elizabeth Prescott, and Lee Walling,* Planning Environments for Young Children: Physical Space, *2nd ed. (Washington, D.C.: National Association for the Education of Young Children, 1977), p. 11.*

Writing tools combined with other materials stimulate use of skills.

materials. Teacher assignments are not required. Teachers can use spatial organization to design settings that stimulate language interaction, shelter a working child, or foster group inquiry. Some aspects of the teacher's work, such as suggesting activities and stimulating idea connections, can be extended through the organization of materials and space. The arranged environment can work in partnership with the teacher's more direct interactions with learners.

Management Tasks

The amount of teacher time that is spent dispensing materials, presiding over routines, and managing child behavior can be minimized when the environment is arranged for that purpose. Some patterns of

Class routines can be environmentally arranged.

spatial organization enable children to work with a minimum of inter-ference and interruption, reducing the need for teacher intervention. Well-organized space and materials smooth independent transitions from one activity to another. Materials organization can foster self-reliance and self-management of children in classroom routines and the care of materials. Administrative procedures like lunch counts, cleanup, and distribution of materials can be carried out through environmental arrangements, instead of taking time. By having a clear grasp of the management possibilities of a well-arranged environment, teachers can free themselves from these and many other tasks that have traditionally consumed much teacher time each day.

Tasks of Environmental Arrangement

The teacher has four major tasks in arranging the basic structure of the learning environment: spatial organization, provisioning for learn-ing, materials arrangement, and organizing for special purposes. Spatial organization is the task of arranging furniture to create spaces for movement and learning activities. Provisioning is the task of selecting, gathering, and making materials and equipment, and placing them in the environment for children's direct access.[8] Materials arrangement is the process of deciding where to place the environments' provisions and how to combine and display them. Organizing for special purposes involves arranging the total environment to promote the instructional purposes of the environment's program. All these tasks combine to produce interacting environmental arrangements that affect most events and behaviors in the environment. At the same time, the way each task is carried out influences a particular group of events most directly.

Spatial Organization

Spatial organization influences much of the movement and physical behaviors of children in the environment. Teachers accomplish this task by defining spaces within the environment, planning traffic patterns, and arranging furniture. Room arrangement is more than a casual responsi-bility or a matter of aesthetics, because spatial organization influences so many behaviors. New spaces are created each time a piece of furniture is put in place, although some of those spaces may not be noticed by the teacher who created them. The spaces and their relationships still in-fluence behavior, whether planned or not.

---

[8]I Do and I Understand, *Nuffield Mathematics Project, vol. 1 (New York: John Wiley & Sons, 1967), 16–17.*

New spaces are created when furniture is moved.

Clear perceptions of the space to be organized, and an understanding of the particular effects of space on movement and activity patterns, are necessary for successful spatial organization. Teachers who perceive classroom space in informed ways can use deliberately organized space to facilitate children's movement and support physical activity for learning.

Provisioning for Learning

Provisioning for learning influences the content and form of learning activities within the environment. As a result, provisioning has a long-term effect on the knowledge, skills, and thinking processes that children can develop as they use the environment. Provisioning influences these outcomes in several different ways. For example, different recording tools elicit different skills, so the teacher's choice of such tools for writing, drawing, and tallying will determine which skills are most practiced. Information sources determine the knowledge content of activities and the skills practiced as children obtain the data offered by the information sources. At the same time, the amount of available information represented by the information sources in the environment determines the depth of children's knowledge and the thinking processes employed in building that knowledge.

Teachers provision by choosing, making, and collecting materials and equipment to support potential activities and explorations of a diverse group of learners. Teachers also make decisions about the timing and context for the introduction of materials for learning.

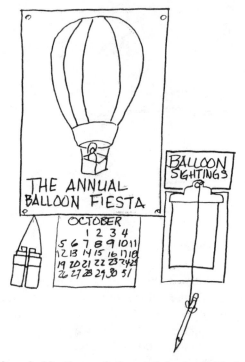

Teachers decide when and where to introduce materials.

Materials Arrangement

Materials arrangement has a strong influence on the students' level of involvement with learning activities. Although arrangement of learning materials is often seen as a housekeeping task, this work is more than establishing an attractive and orderly room. Many different classroom events are caused by materials arrangement, some related to management and behavior and others to the breadth and depth of learning in the environment. Attention span, the variety of skills elicited by the environment, and the materials most used or most ignored are all influenced by materials arrangement.[9]

The teacher carries out the materials arrangement task through careful organization and display of learning materials, and location of materials for learner access. Deliberate decisions about the location and distribution of learning materials throughout the environment, so as to stimulate interest and suggest learning activities, are also part of this task.

[9]*Margaret Skutch and Wilfred Hamlin,* To Start a School *(Boston: Little, Brown, 1971), pp. 3–11.*

Teachers display learning materials to stimulate interest.

Organizing for Special Purposes

Organizing for special purposes is the environmental task that employs all the teacher's knowledge of environmental arrangements and classroom events. Using all the principles available for designing an effective environment, the teacher chooses those arrangements most likely to meet the needs of individuals and the teacher's particular purposes for children's learning. This requires both a clear understanding of environmental principles and a clarification of desired learning outcomes, behavior expectations, and learner needs.[10]

[10]*Loughlin, "Understanding the Learning Environment," p. 125.*

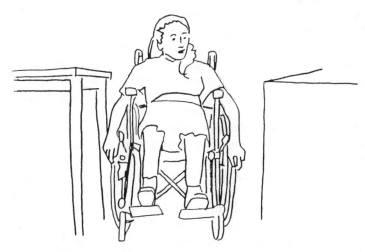

Environments are organized to meet special purposes.

Building a Conceptual View of Environment

To carry out the major tasks of arranging the learning environment, the teacher must have a conceptual framework about the active and influencing nature of the environment and its relationship to learning. Developing a conceptual framework calls for a particular way of looking at learning space and of solving problems, rather than a set of procedures or recipes for arranging the environment.

An important starting place for this conceptual task is the sorting out of elements that are often combined in an undifferentiated, conglomerate view of environment. Differentiating these elements doesn't mean choosing between them, but increasing the precision with which each is considered. Thinking clearly about these elements of the learning environment is a good basis for the working principles that guide environmental arrangement.

Subject Matter and Behavior

Planning, organizing, and provisioning seem to be ever-present teaching tasks. Each requires some knowledge base to give direction, establish purposes, clarify problems, and identify potential solutions. In the past, the analysis of subject matter has been a common framework for thinking about all events in the classroom. Subject-matter perspectives have shaped the selection of instructional materials and teaching strategies, each designed to promote specific concepts or skills. Learning activities, classroom centers, and interpretation of children's statements and actions have also been regarded from this subject-centered view of curriculum.

A different perspective is traditionally used by professionals who design environments to support the activities of people who occupy them. Using behavior as a base, the architect considers the movements and activities that will occur, the materials or equipment they will use, and necessary access to other spaces. The relationship of the physical behaviors of people to structural space determines the design developed for a room, a building, or a landscape.

Both perspectives offer important tools for teachers as they carry out their planning, organizing, and provisioning tasks. It is important to be clear about the specific environmental problems for which each offers direction. A subject-matter base offers direction for only a part of the environmental work of the teacher: the selection of information sources and some basic tools for recording and processing that information. An analysis of important concepts or skills for the learner will influence, but not limit, the variety of information sources and the choice of specific

Space facilitates the physical actions of learners.

data that children will encounter as they use them. It will also influence the selection of tools and information sources for eliciting particular skills and processes.

Most of the teacher's work with the arranged environment requires the organizing of spaces and materials to support the physical actions of learners as they go about their work. A behavior base is the appropriate analysis tool for this task. It isn't useful to think about the organization of space in terms of concepts to be taught, or ideas to be learned, since the function of space is to facilitate the physical movement, groupings, and actions of children. Children observe, build, chart, measure, or carry water; they don't arithmetic, science, or phonic.[11]

A behavior base for planning the arranged environment means asking crucial questions about physical actions. How many children will occupy the space at one time? Will they sit, stand, move about? Will they talk, work cooperatively, work independently? How large is the equipment or material they will handle? Will they use electrical outlets? Will they stack, pile, or sort objects? Will they write, read, or calculate on paper? Will they need to gather materials, moving in and out of the space? Will they stay in the space or carry materials away? Such questions will help the teacher arrange successful environments.

Designing Activities and Offering Materials

As teachers provision the environment for spontaneous learning activities and teacher-planned experiences, there are two basic pro-

[11]*Nancy M. Rambusch, "Helping Children Become Self-Directive and Self-Selective" (Paper presented at the Annual Meeting of the National Association for the Education of Young Children, Minneapolis, November 1971).*

Materials can suggest activities without limiting options.

visioning patterns available: provisioning by designing activities and provisioning by offering materials.

When the teachers provide a set of materials with a predetermined use or for one specific activity, they are designing activities as they provision. Setting up learning centers or interest centers usually requires designing the specific activity for which the materials are to be used.[12] Provisioning by designing activities makes some demands upon the teacher. It is necessary to explain to learners the nature of the activity and procedures they must follow, which requires the presence of the teacher, or teacher instructions in task cards or some other form. Without clarification, learners are likely to use the material in ways the teacher did not intend.

When materials are set out for learner access, with no particular stipulation other than ground rules about the activities for which they may be used, teachers provision by offering materials. The particular arrangement or combinations of materials can suggest activities without limiting other possibilities. Materials are available to support the work that arises spontaneously within the framework of ongoing learning activities. Provisioning by offering materials makes demands upon the teachers. Learning materials must be considered in terms of qualities that create potential for multiple activities and support a variety of learnings. This requires seeing materials in quite a different way from conventional, single-purpose views of instructional materials.

[12]*Ann b. Piechowiak and Myra B. Cook,* Complete Guide to the Elementary Learning Center *(West Nyack, N.Y.: Parker Publishing, 1976), pp. 70–73.*

It is important for teachers to be aware, when placing materials in the environment, whether the intent is to design activities or to offer materials. Some balance between the two is necessary to help learners develop and to limit the size of the teacher's task as well. When the balance leans heavily toward designing activities, the opportunities for learners to structure their own learning situation from within are severely limited.[13] At the same time, a teacher's task of personally inventing all possibilities for learning activities that can occur in the environment is demanding and time-consuming.

Learning Materials and Material Holders

Learning materials and the material holders are the parts of the arranged environment most likely to be gathered, made, or assembled by teachers. Therefore teachers determine the appearance and form of many learning materials, and of most of the holders and organizers containing the materials.

Learning materials are the objects that children handle, manipulate, or otherwise incorporate into their learning experiences. Materials in the environment stimulate learning by providing information and suggesting activities. How well the material can do this depends on its setting and on the way it is displayed. Material holders are the boxes, baskets, trays, and shelving that teachers use to organize and arrange the materials for children's access. Highly decorated holders can focus visual attention upon themselves, but can also camouflage the learning materials they contain.

It is important to consider learning materials as distinct from their containers when making decisions about the arrangement of materials for learning. When selecting and preparing holders to display materials, teachers must place the visual focus on the learning material rather than on the material holders. It is not, after all, the boxes that provide the

[13]*Alice Yardley,* Structure in Early Learning *(New York: Citation Press, 1974),* pp. 1–9.

Visual focus is on the materials; not their holders.

information and the stimulus for learning, but the learning materials themselves.

Child Environment and Adult Environment

Because of differences in sizes, roles, movement patterns, and experience backgrounds, the visual and spatial experiences of adults and children in the learning environment are not the same. Children and adults in the same room occupy different space, see different surroundings, and perceive the contents of the environment differently.

The children's environment consists of the spaces they can occupy, the materials they can see and reach. It includes also the spaces, materials, paths, and information perceived as they move through the environment or scan it visually. The children's environment doesn't include the space above their heads, or any of the surfaces or objects it contains. For most elementary school children a bookcase four feet high functions as a wall. So the child's environment doesn't include an overview of the total environment with its subdivisions of space. As they scan or move through the environment, children may perceive a great deal of printed material without perceiving it as information.

The adults' environment consists of the space they can observe or occupy, the materials they can see and reach, and also the stored

**Teachers should perceive the children's environment
from the children's eye level.**

materials organized out of sight. It includes all spaces, materials, movement, paths, and information that the adults can perceive as they scan or move through the environment. Adults can perceive print information, an overview of the total environment, and objects or surfaces two to three feet above eye level. The adults' environment doesn't include the vertical surfaces or spaces with entrances below knee level, or walls four feet high blocking vision of spaces or paths.

The distinction between the adult environment and the child environment is an important one. In order to predict likely behaviors as children operate in the learning environment, teachers must remove themselves from the adult environment so as to enter the child's environment and perceive space, materials, and information as the child does. Teachers can do this only by positioning themselves in the places where children work and move, and by scanning the environment from the child's eye level. Only then can the teacher understand the effects of environmental arrangements on the learners. [14]

Environmental Analysis to Solve Problems

The learning environment influences behaviors in many different ways. Environmental messages urge movement, call attention to some learning materials but not others, encourage deep or superficial involvement, invite children to hurry or move calmly. Environmental arrangements can also promote independence and self-direction, encourage use of skills, and lengthen or shorten the attention span. With or without teacher awareness, the environment sends messages and learners respond. The influence of the environment is continuous and pervasive, regardless of the program style or behavior expectations of the teacher. A conceptual view of the environment offers tools that teachers can use to recognize a number of environmentally caused problems.

Environmental problems can be analyzed in two ways: as problems of commission or omission. It is possible to describe some behavior and events as problems of commission associated with particular patterns of spatial organization, provisioning, or materials arrangement. With a beginning understanding of these associations, a teacher can easily recognize physical interference, excessive traffic, or lost and ruined materials as environmentally caused. These and other behaviors and events may be generated by the environment.

It is a more demanding task to recognize problems of omission— inadequacies in the learning environment revealed by events that fail to occur. When children don't write because the materials for writing are

[14]*Kritchevsky, Prescott, and Walling,* Planning Environments, *p. 18.*

stored out of sight and out of reach, and nobody is asking questions about the water cycle during the rainy season because there is no visible stimulus to inquiry in that area, the environment is inadequate. The same is true if nobody is reading library books because the library is behind a screen, and if nobody is showing interest in the plants on the windowsill because there are no accompanying tools, materials, or information to encourage repotting, identification, propagation, or recording growth under various conditions.

Identification and analysis of problems of omission require a clear and well-developed understanding of the potential power of the environment. Frequent observations and analysis of the environment and associated behavior are necessary for this understanding. Teachers must analyze classroom events by asking themselves such questions as "What possible environmental arrangements could be creating this behavior?" and "What changes in the environment could cause new and desired behaviors to appear?"

The discussions in the following chapters are organized around the tasks of the teacher in establishing the arranged environment. This information, and the principles of environmental organization described, all reflect the conceptual view of the learning environment presented here, which in turn rests upon a clear understanding of the elements of environment and the environment-behavior relationship.

Observations of environment and associated behaviors are important.

SECTION I

ORGANIZATION OF SPACE

CHAPTER 2

FINDING SPACE FOR LEARNING

No matter what kinds of architectural facility teachers are given to work in, finding space for learning seems to be a perpetual task. Activity patterns change as students gain competencies and new spaces are needed to fit those patterns. The room arrangement that organized space very well at the beginning of the year doesn't work so well as the year progresses. As teachers search for new space to accommodate learning activities, the environment often seems too small, or too cut up, or the wrong shape. Built-in features may seem to allow too few choices for alternative arrangements.

But in almost every learning environment undeveloped learning spaces have been overlooked by the teacher, and there are other spaces that aren't being used much. Neglected learning space remains undeveloped because of teacher perceptions of space. Habitual ways of seeing and thinking about classrooms often interfere with the teacher's ability to visualize arrangement possibilities making use of that overlooked and undeveloped learning space. If space is ignored by students, usually it means that classroom space has been seen and planned from the teacher's, not the learner's, perspective.

If teachers can set aside some habitual but unconscious ways of looking at space and considering its organization, they can rediscover all the space the environment has to offer for learning activities. Shifting to the student's perspective on space makes it easier to organize spaces that can support children's work comfortably and help them feel at ease in the environment.

The Too-Small Classroom

Day after day, dozens of problems with bumping, crowding, and jostling appeared in the classroom where Louise Garcia and Jack

Helmholz worked with third graders. Both teachers spent a lot of time helping children settle down to work after each interruption. All day Louise and Jack listened to children's complaints: Alfredo knocked Paul's art project off his desk when he passed by on the way to his math group; children's elbows got in one another's way at the reading group; Marcia said she couldn't see to do her seat work, because everybody kept standing in front of the chalkboard; and Angelica was sure that tall Roberto had pushed his feet out in front of his desk just to trip her as she walked by to sharpen her pencil. The classroom was simply too small. Toward the end of the day the principal sent word that two more children were enrolling, and Louise marched down to the office to tell the principal it would be impossible to put two more children in the room. She insisted the principal come and look.

Every day there were dozens of problems with crowding.

In the environment, the principal listened to the two teachers describe the overcrowding. Then she moved about, looking from several different locations, stooping down to children's height to look again. She asked the teachers if they had ever considered rearranging the environment to relieve the crowding. They assured her they had tried every pattern of desk arrangement possible, from tablelike groupings to semicircles, back-to-front rows, and a large T-formation. None of these relieved the crowding at all. Clearly, the classroom was too small.

In a roomy area near the doorway, the principal saw a bookcase, a teacher's desk, a large table, and a tall storage cabinet. The teachers explained that this area, and another like it across the room, were their own reserved work places, needed to prepare materials for teaching, to plan, and to store instructional materials. No, these areas weren't available for children's use.

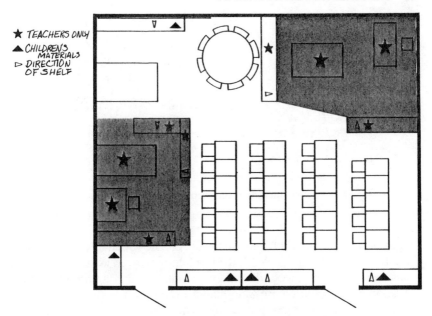

★ TEACHERS ONLY
▲ CHILDREN'S MATERIALS
▷ DIRECTION OF SHELF

Rearranging the desks didn't relieve the crowding.

During the school day the teachers spent most of their time in the small group instruction areas, where each worked directly with children on lessons or projects. The children spent their days at assigned desks, or in the small group areas where they worked with a teacher two or three times a day. If the classroom were larger, the teachers pointed out, they could set up other special areas where children could have something beside seat work to do. Meanwhile the teachers were preparing enough work to keep everybody occupied and doing their best to cope with the inadequate space.

The principal and the teachers talked again about the teachers' personal work places and why they needed them. The teachers said there wasn't time to use them when the children were in the room; they used them before or after school. Now the principal walked through the environment again, and this time she moved in and out of the teachers' areas, looking around from children's height. She suggested that the three of them think together again about classroom space, first making some measurements so they would all know the size of the space they were talking about.

The teachers measured the room dimensions and made some quick calculations of area, while the principal measured and calculated the amount of space reserved for the teachers. When they compared their

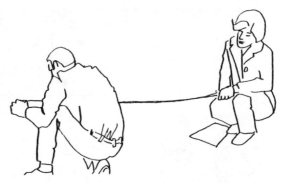

The teachers measured the room and calculated the areas.

figures, Louise and Jack were astonished. They suddenly realized why the room was too small. With the teachers' reserved areas, which were unused during the school day, they had taken nearly a third of the total available space out of use, and had crowded the learning environment into the tight two-thirds remaining. Then, without realizing it, every time they tried to rearrange the classroom, they acted as though the space occupied by teacher work areas didn't exist. They continued to organize a too-small classroom within a much larger physical space. It suddenly dawned on them that if the space of their reserved areas were used for learning activities during the day, it would still be available before and after school for planning and preparation. They could rearrange the classroom so that all the space and furniture were organized as children's learning space, thus enlarging the classroom and offering more flexibility for the day's work and movement.

Visualizing Classroom Space

The real problem with many too-small classrooms is not so much their actual sizes, but the way teachers look at them, seeing only part of the available space and overlooking the rest. When furniture is placed in an environment, it affects the appearance of the overall space available, highlighting some and camouflaging some, so that it is difficult to visualize the space as it looked when empty. After the environment is arranged, it is still difficult to see spaces that haven't been assigned for special purposes, but much easier to see spaces like painting areas or reading group settings that are set up for particular activities. Although all teachers don't see classroom space in exactly the same way, there are some common problems in visualizing it clearly. Some kinds of spaces are more likely to be invisible to teachers' eyes than others. Those are the areas that are most often neglected in spatial organization.

Seeing Teacher Space as Learning Space

The teachers who worked in the too-small classroom forgot about two large areas that could have been used for children's learning, because they saw the edges of their own work areas as walls. For some reason, they acted as though children and teachers could never use the same spaces for work, even though they didn't use those spaces at the same times. Once they had set the boundaries of their own work areas, it was as if that space had disappeared. Even though they desperately needed more usable space, those teacher areas stayed off limits and unused throughout the whole school day.

Many learning environments would seem larger if teachers and children shared all the space. Table space can be provisioned for children's activity with materials arranged in holders that are also carriers; it takes just a moment each morning to provision the table. The same work area is available for teachers' work when the holders with children's provisions are temporarily removed, and teachers' tools and materials in their carrier are set out. Even the teacher's desk can become a work surface during the school day, if children's provisions are organized so they can be easily moved at the end of the day. Organizers for the teacher's materials are also helpful for quick changes from child space to teacher space.

It takes just a moment to provision a table for children.

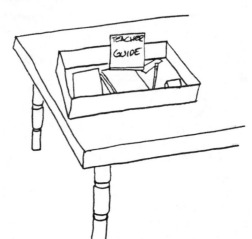

The materials can be changed for teacher's work.

The teacher's desk can be a work surface.

Looking Beyond the Real Classroom

When a classroom is arranged with assigned seats for each child, a teacher is apt to see the Real Classroom as the area where the desks or tables are grouped, while viewing the remaining spaces in the back or around the edges as leftover space. The activities of the day are crowded into that main part of the environment, and leftover space is used for learning activities only occasionally or not at all. When teachers look at their environments and see just the Real Classroom, they forget that those other spaces along the walls are also part of the environment. Perhaps this way of seeing space explains why there are so many classrooms with bookshelves lined up along the walls. The teachers who use this arrangement often explain that placing shelves at right angles to the wall would make them extend into the classroom. They haven't noticed that the shelves are already in the classroom, because to their eyes the wall space is not in the Real Classroom. If that leftover space were organized and provisioned for use, the classroom would seem much larger and offer more space for learning.

Visualizing More than Four Corners

There are all sorts of overlooked spaces in classrooms that could house libraries, art projects, reading groups, or other specialized activities. When a teacher looks around for sheltered spaces to set up special activity areas and sees only the room's four corners, it's easy to believe there aren't enough spaces available. But there are ways to create small areas with two-sided shelter in places that aren't room corners. Furniture arrangements beside classroom walls and in little-used spaces closer to the center of the environment can add corners and increase the space available for learning.

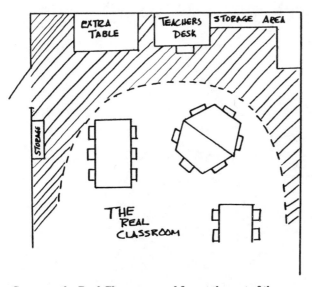

Some see the Real Classroom and forget the rest of the space.

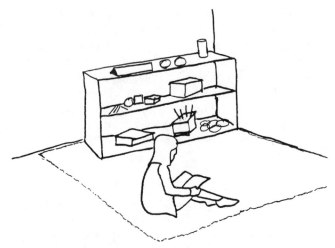

A shelf unit along the wall doesn't define space.

A movable shelf unit, lined up along the wall near a corner, offers materials for use in that corner but doesn't provide any space divisions. When the same shelf unit is turned so it is at right angles to the wall, an additional corner is created that can be provisioned for special activities.

Dividers can create corners in the center of space. The furniture that defines a central corner is usually low enough not to block views, and long enough to clarify the corner's boundaries. Also, children some-

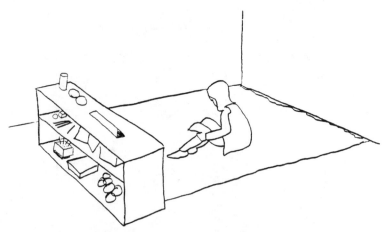

Placed at right angles to the wall, the shelf unit makes another corner.

Low dividers can make corners in the center of the room.

times find their own corners between fairly large pieces of furniture; such spaces can be provisioned to become undisturbed working places for individuals. Shelf units placed at various angles to one another can create corners away from classroom walls, while at the same time holding provisions for activities in those new corners. And the backs of cabinets, pianos, and teachers' desks can be the beginnings of corners; each needs just another side to define and shelter a working area.

Children can find their own corners.

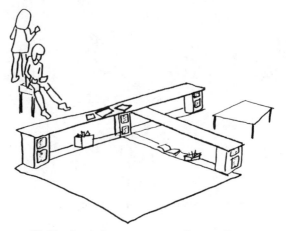

Shelf units make corners away from walls.

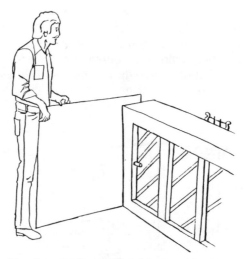

Furniture backs are the beginnings of corners.

Discovering Small Unseen Spaces

Some spaces are more easily overlooked than others. The edges of a classroom, space near permanent lockers or coat hooks, floor space between two facing doors on opposite walls, or space beyond the doorway near the back corner of the classroom — all these are often unseen. Arrangements to define and provision such spaces could enlarge the apparent size of many classrooms that seem crowded.

A strip of floor space seems small, but it's enough for one child.

Sometimes children find their own small places where they can work quietly. A narrow strip of floor space beyond the doorway seems too small to notice, but there can be enough space for a child to settle down with a book. And places for very small groups can be arranged in the space between opposite doorways; chart racks, screens, or other dividers can establish the spaces, without interfering with clear paths to the doorways.

Places for very small groups can be arranged between opposite doorways.

Old Ideas About Room Arrangement

Even when teachers can visualize space clearly, they may have difficulty considering new ideas about spatial organization, having always thought about room arrangement in certain traditional ways. These habits of thinking may come from the classrooms of their childhood or from past teaching experiences, but rarely reflect conscious views of environment. Teachers who recognize these thinking patterns and then approach the organization of space with fresh views, often find arrangement possibilities and spatial flexibility that they have never considered before.

Thinking It Must Be All the Same

Some teachers act as though using one piece of furniture in a particular way means that every other piece of furniture like it should be used in precisely the same way. Thus all tables are reserved for working on paper and pencil assignments; all desks are placed in rows or tables or circles or solitary arrangements; all desks and tables are massed in one part of the room; all the shelving is lined up along the walls. A more flexible arrangement of space and furniture might serve children's learning activities more effectively, but thinking in the All framework

Attaching small wheels to a shelf unit makes it easy to shift.

A group area could have a low divider along the center.

makes it hard to consider some desks in a short row, some in a table group, some paired, or some arranged alone in specially provisioned areas.

In some environments, several times a week children all need to be seated at a writing surface at the same time and to see the same chalkboard. So the teacher arranges the tables in a group and leaves them that way all the time, even though the children could do much of their work in other places. In other classrooms an area for a class meeting is needed for a few minutes each day, so a large empty space is reserved for that purpose all the time, even though smaller spaces for learning activities are urgently needed during the rest of the day. If arrangements were more flexible, they could be changed for short-term use, shifting from small, much-needed working spaces to a larger single area used now and then for everybody.

It's easy to attach small wheels or casters to a shelf unit. A screwdriver, perhaps a drill, and a set of casters is all it takes. Furniture on wheels can be used to divide large spaces into smaller areas. It takes just a few moments to shift wheeled furniture so as to provide a large space for short-term use.

A large group area for presentation and story reading can sometimes be arranged with a low divider along the center; children on either side of the divider can still see, hear, and participate. At different times of the day, however, the same work area can shelter small groups of children planning or discussing projects. No furniture shifting is needed for either use of the space.

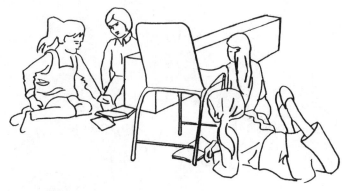

The same work area shelters small groups at work.

The Middle of the Room

The Middle of the Room is a special case of the All approach to room arrangement. Something about it makes it hard for many teachers to consider its possibilities in the same way they think about the rest of the classroom. Although other spaces may be divided into well-defined and provisioned areas, the Middle of the Room often remains a large and homogeneous space. It may be filled with desks or tables, or left empty. Such arrangements leave only the perimeters of the environment for organization into smaller areas for special purposes.

Potentially, the Middle of the Room is learning space like any other space in the environment. A teacher can organize space by establishing one or two special provisioned areas in the central spaces first, then

A special area can be arranged in the center.

The middle of the room can become a message center.

design spatial organization in relation to those areas. By initially dividing the Middle of the Room into several spaces, the teacher will grasp the possibilities of a larger proportion of classroom space than otherwise.

An area provisioned for special purposes can be established in the center of the environment. Low dividers or shelf units define the space without blocking vision. The middle of the room is a good location for a message and bulletin center; routines, schedules, and other notices are then available for frequent reference during the day. Tall furniture can be useful there for defining work areas and paths; its length may block

Tall furniture is useful for defining paths.

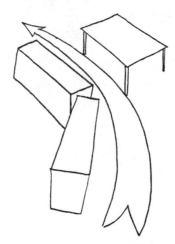

A diagonal arrangement establishes paths.

vision in one but not in all directions. Diagonal furniture placed in the center of the environment also establishes paths and work areas, and gives the space a different feeling.

Thinking About Seating First

In some learning environments it is considered important for every child to have a special desk or table, while in others personal ownership of these spaces is not important. In some classrooms there are times when every child needs to be seated at a table or desk space; in others, the use of places for work changes and flows all day long. Different styles of organization tend to create different patterns of seating that help set the design for the rest of the classroom space.

When permanent seating for every child is a priority in classroom arrangement, spatial organization often begins with the placement of desks or tables, and further organization revolves around the permanent seating. When all the permanent seating is clustered in one area, considerable space is needed for the separation of desks or tables, so children can move into and out of their seats. Other furniture that could define spaces and hold materials is then arranged away from the cluster of desks or tables, and even more spaces between furniture are needed, so children can walk about to get materials. Although most of these spaces arranged for movement may be small, together they remove quite a bit of potential learning space from use. The space left for developing and provisioning smaller learning areas is quite limited.

There are many flexible ways to provide special seating for everyone. Spaces can be used in more than one way, at different times, and by

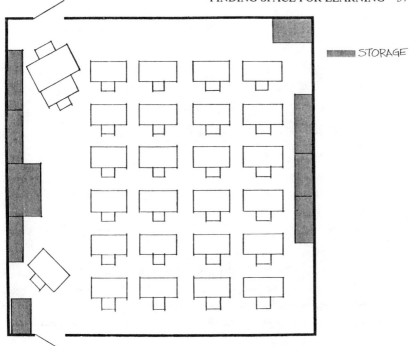

STORAGE

Much total space is used to separate desks and make room for movement.

different people, and materials can be arranged close to work spaces. Planning for room arrangement can begin with the division and organization of all the available space for multiple purposes, then seating can be arranged within those spaces. Some teachers who find special seating important disperse tables or desks throughout the environment, so that each functions in some defined and provisioned learning space. Yet the seating is also available for those times when it seems necessary for every child to be seated at once. In such environments, providing places for work is part of spatial organization, instead of a separate process.

Thinking About Carpet as Boundaries

For some reason, the edges of permanently installed carpeting are often treated as solid barriers when furniture is arranged. If the carpet covers just one area along a wall, the furniture is apt to be arranged along the edges. When the carpeted area is much larger and centrally located, its edges may become the boundaries of the Real Classroom with its formal seating areas, while the uncarpeted areas are left for other uses. But carpet is, after all, just floor space. It may often be useful to take

Furniture can be placed across the edges of a carpet.

advantage of the softness and quietness that carpet offers, but this doesn't mean carpeted space can't be divided into smaller areas for learning activities. Furniture can be placed across the edges of carpeting, so that spaces are defined by the furniture rather than the carpet. Some of the carpeted floor can be included with uncarpeted floor space in defined and provisioned areas, and smaller pieces of the carpeted floor can be arranged into quiet work spaces for small groups or individuals.

Thinking Furniture Must Be Parallel

In some learning environments, especially those that are rectangular, teachers seem to think it necessary to square off the furniture arrangement. Everything is lined up along the nearest wall or arranged parallel to one wall or another, even when the furniture is some distance from any wall.

But diagonal placement of some furniture can produce effective space divisions in the environment. Sometimes the diagonal arrangement brings more space into use, as a different focus and definition reveal new small spaces for learning. The definition of paths is often improved by changing the angle of a shelf or cabinet. The sense of enclosure of some areas is increased, and openings into other areas are clarified. Shifting space-defining furniture to a diagonal arrangement here or there in the environment also softens the hard edges of the right angles of parallel placement. Flexible thinking about furniture alignment offers greater variety in working places, and can help make better use of more classroom space.

Thinking Built-ins Are Special

Built-in features of the environment are often regarded as very special, never to be altered or blocked. Perceived this way, they can dictate the spatial organization of an environment, often cutting off

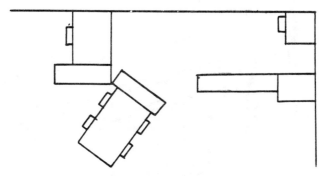

Diagonal furniture arrangement makes a variety of spaces.

several feet of usable room space. The unused space is left in front of each built-in, for access to its storage.

But there are other ways to think about built-ins. In some instances they can be dismantled and moved to other locations. When they must remain in place and more learning space is needed, it may be better to block off part of a built-in bookcase than to have access to every inch of shelving. It may be necessary to temporarily disregard built-ins, in order to plan spatial organization that includes all the environment's space. After the basic spatial organization has been designed, the teacher can find ways to make use of as much built-in equipment as possible within that design, but not at the expense of adequate space for learning activities.

Tables can be placed against a built-in shelf unit without destroying all of its storage capacity. Students then have access to some segments of the shelving, whose upper levels can hold materials needed at the table.

A table can be placed against a built-in shelf unit.

Space directly in front of closed cabinets can be used for learning activities.

The space in front of closed cabinets can be used for learning activity in the same way other space is used. To avoid interruption of learning activities, the built-ins can be used for long-term storage, so there is no need to open cabinet doors during the day. Access is possible when the environment isn't in use. Furthermore, built-ins can sometimes help define space, or be incorporated into activity areas that make use of their special features.

Space from the Child's Perspective

Children in a learning environment sometimes avoid particular spaces, while other spaces that look no more attractive to the teacher appear to be in great demand. Certain areas are the site of quarreling and tensions that don't appear in others. Children seem to focus on tasks better in some locations than in others that the teacher sees as equally quiet. When carefully organized and provisioned spaces don't function well, they aren't useful. New spatial organization may be needed to make these areas more useful, but the teacher needs to understand why the spaces aren't working as expected.

Many events can be understood only when teachers see the environment from the learners' perspective. Some of this can be done by physically moving down into the spaces children occupy and looking about from their eye level. At times a teacher must learn how space is used in the child's community and observe individual children's use of space. There are other times when understanding the effects of spatial organization requires imagining oneself in the child's position in order to understand the harmony or dissonance between environmental suggestions and teacher demands.

Built-ins can be incorporated into activity areas.

Looking from the Child's Eye Level

There is considerable difference between space seen from adult height and its appearance from lower eye levels. In almost every learning environment arranged for children, adults can understand the suggestions, effects, and behavioral invitations of spatial organization only from children's eye level and locations. Many otherwise puzzling events become understandable in this way, including scant use of some well-developed learning spaces, when access routes are not visible from children's eye level.

The effects of natural light in environments with windows, or of artificial lighting in other places, are different from adults' and children's viewpoints. Light patterns that create glare and discomfort from the

From child's eye level, teachers can see why some spaces are little used.

child's position may not be evident from adult height, or even from child height at all times of the day. Lighting that might cause obvious problems for children who stay in the same location and position all day, is less apt to cause problems in more flexible arrangements where children have access to all the environment's work spaces and move from place to place throughout the day. To understand the effects of lighting patterns for children, the teacher must look from within their spaces at the times of day when children are most likely to use those spaces.

Observing Space Use

Many children prefer some places to others, because the spatial arrangements in those areas reflect the way space is used in their own lives and communities. In less familiar spaces they may move furniture, when they can, into arrangements that feel more comfortable. Children may push desks closer together to be within touching distance of friends, or hitch their chairs nearer to the teacher in reading groups. Children from cultures in which communication includes physical touching and close conversational space may be uncomfortable in settings that demand greater conversational distances and permit minimal physical contact.[1] Groups of children from some socioeconomic settings seem to function productively in relatively congested space where children from different settings may become irritable and quarrelsome.[2]

Teachers can understand how spatial messages are interpreted by the individuals in the learning environment by observing children's personal use of space. They can observe children's movements towards or away from others in close space; the amount of space a child claims for materials being used in an activity; the kinds of spaces selected when choice is given; and the amount of intrusion an individual can accept without becoming restless. Time spent in the child's community, observing the way space is used there, helps a teacher understand children's past experiences with space. Seeing classroom space from the student's viewpoint offers insights for developing spaces children can use productively.

Seeing Oneself in the Child's Place

Another way to look at space from the child's perspective is for teachers to imagine themselves in the settings where children work, and

[1]*Joan C. Dye, "Relationship of 'Life-Space' to Human Aggression: Implications for the Teacher in Bilingual-Bicultural Education,"* in The Bilingual Child, ed. *Antonio Simoes (New York: Academic Press, 1976), pp. 173–88.*

[2]*Sybil Kritchevsky, Elizabeth Prescott, and Lee Walling,* Planning Environments for Young Children: Physical Space, *2nd ed. (Washington, D.C.: National Association for the Education of Young Children, 1977), pp. 34–36.*

Children push desks together to be closer to their friends.

to consider the invitations those settings may offer. This is especially helpful for trying to understand the relationship between behavior messages of particular spaces, in contrast to the teacher's expectations for behavior in those same spaces. Insights, for instance into the effects of social space and private space on children's behavior, aren't difficult to develop, with a shift to the child's perspective. These insights can help teachers develop learning spaces that support children's efforts to meet behavior expectations.

Any behavioral setting that places people so they face one another around a table or in a circle of chairs, invites social interaction such as chatting and visiting. If the table is also provisioned, people around the table are encouraged to participate in some common shared activity with those materials and to talk about it. Private space, in contrast, shelters individuals from the stimulation of others, and makes it easier for children to focus on demanding individual tasks.[3] Looking at spatial organization from the child's perspective helps the teacher realize that children who are working in social spaces have great difficulty behaving as though they were in private space. Teachers who understand this can organize space to take advantage of small areas, developing private spaces in places that might seem too small for groups of children.

Checking Your Own Environment

Are there areas of space in your environment not used for learning activities? You can see this by looking at your classroom without furniture, then with the furniture in its current arrangement. You can

---

[3]*Elizabeth Jones,* Dimensions of Teaching-Learning Environments: Handbook for Teachers *(Pasadena: Pacific Oaks College Bookstore, 1973), p. 15.*

identify those areas of the environment that children can use, and spaces that aren't developed for student use. Trying out some alternate arrangements will help you visualize the space more clearly.

It's much easier to experiment with spatial organization by manipulating two-dimensional drawings of furniture on a floor plan drawn to scale, than to push furniture around every time an arrangement is tried out. The floor plan and furniture drawings are not difficult to prepare, and they make it possible to try out a large number of arrangements in a fairly short time.

1. The first step in making a floor plan to scale is accurate measurement. Measure and record the dimensions of the environment and locations and sizes of everything permanently built-in. There may be larger cabinets and structures that have stayed in a traditional location since the room was first furnished, but these are not to be drawn on the floor plan. They may offer options for space arrangement when they are recognized as freestanding.
2. With the measurements as reference, draw the floor plan with all its permanent features. The scale needs to be large enough so furniture drawings are easy to handle, but not so large that the floor plan is unwieldy. With a half-inch scale (½ inch = 1 foot), most learning environments can be drawn on a sheet of 16″ × 22″ paper. Quarter-inch graph paper makes drawing to this scale fairly easy.
3. To draw the furniture, take accurate measurements of every piece in the environment. Measure the largest width and depth of each piece, usually around the foot or base. Then draw furniture silhouettes to the same scale used on the floor plan. Cutting the drawings from dark construction paper will make the furniture pieces show clearly against the lighter floor plan. Include every piece of furniture because everything, including chairs, stools, bookracks, and floor cushions, consumes space. Each individual piece must be represented to give a realistic picture of spaces, paths, and room for activity in the environment.
4. Move the furniture pieces of the floor plan to represent your current arrangement, but don't fasten them down.
5. Examine your arrangement carefully. While considering all the space, examine the uses of the areas within the environment.
   — What spaces are always available for children?
   — Which spaces are occasionally used by children?
   — Which spaces are seldom used by children?
   — Which spaces are never available for children?
   — Are there crowded spaces? Does the congestion vary with time?

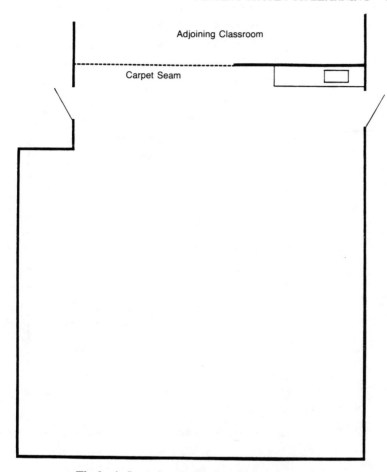

Adjoining Classroom

Carpet Seam

The basic floor plan shows all built-in features.

— Which spaces are used by children for traffic?
— Which spaces are used by children to settle down?

   If you find that children spend their time in only part of the environment and that some areas aren't used at all, you may want to reconsider your arrangement of space. Perhaps a different arrangement could incorporate the unused space into the work and activities of the day. If you find that all the space was used at least part of the time, you may want to consider whether the patterns of use support children's learning effectively. Don't be too disappointed if you discover some

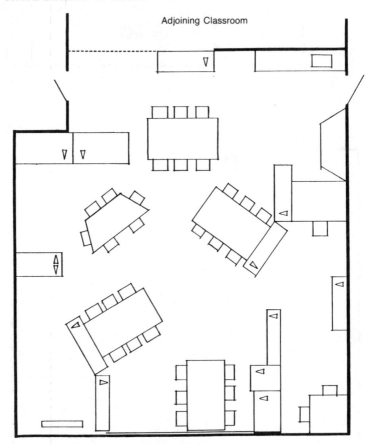

A trial arrangement of furniture on the basic floor plan.

space you'd forgotten to develop: it's a nice way to find a larger classroom than you thought you had. And the floor plan and furniture set will be a useful tool as you continue to study your learning environment closely.

CHAPTER 3

ORGANIZING SPACE IN THE ENVIRONMENT

Organizing space in the learning environment begins with furniture arrangement, which divides the total area of the classroom into smaller spaces. Some spaces are designed by the teacher but others, created without intent, may be unnoticed. Because spatial organization influences actions and other behaviors, the unnoticed spaces may either support or contradict the teacher's purposes and expectations for children's behavior.

The Space in the Middle of the Room

Carol Lovato thought that the beginning of each kindergarten day should be a pleasant experience for the children and for the teacher, too. She wanted each session to begin with conversation and songs in the large group area. The kindergarten environment was a large one, providing plenty of space for the active learning style of the five-year-olds. Carol had arranged the furniture so there would always be space for large group activities and movement in the center of the room. A series of divided and sheltered areas along the walls of the room opened to the center space, which also served as the main traffic route from one place to another.

At one end of the room stood two large shelf units, angled into a V-shape and facing the center space. The shelf units created a traffic route along the backs and around the ends of the shelving. The large group area was at the opposite end of the environment, beside the piano. The strong, clear lines of the furniture placement led children directly into a large, empty center space (see figure on page 48).

47

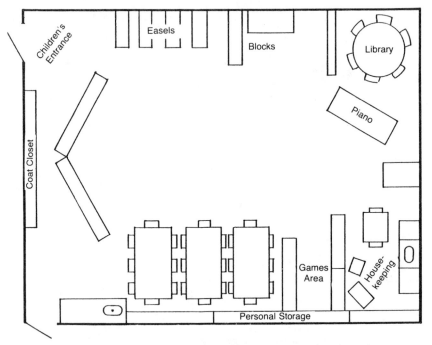

A strong path led children into the large center.

Each morning and afternoon, the children entered the kindergarten from the playground and hung their outdoor clothing and other belongings in the closet behind the shelf units. Coming away from the closet, the children turned to look over the tops of the shoulder-high shelf units to see the other people. Carol moved with the early arrivals across the room to the piano, where they visited and waited to greet others entering the area.

The teacher's expectations for the children's behavior at this time of the day were consistent, and the children were often told of those expectations. Each child should cross the room from the coat closet to the piano area quietly and calmly, then settle down with the group for the morning or afternoon get-together.

Instead, except for the one or two early arrivals who crossed the space with the teacher, and a few others, some very different behaviors occurred. The children moved behind the shelf units, around the ends, and into the center area, where the space seemed to overcome them. They began to hurry. This led to running, with some friendly chasing and wrestling. There was occasional sliding over the waxed tile floor. Some of the children eventually arrived at the other side of the room by

In the center space, some very different behaviors occurred.

themselves, but many needed to be called firmly, reminded, nagged, or pushed along to get across the space to the piano.

Carol wanted the children's first experience each day to be positive, a time of sharing. But instead, she found herself nagging, calling, refereeing, and reciting the rules again and again: "No running! No wrestling! Come directly to the piano!" Despite all the scolding, the beginning of each session continued to be hectic, with everybody behaving in ways they hadn't intended. It wasn't very pleasant.

Something seemed to happen to children in the center space at other times of the day, too. Carol found herself constantly reminding and redirecting children as they moved out of one area into the middle of the room on the way to another activity. Once in the center space, they seemed to forget where they were going, and to be unable to move into

Carol found herself constantly reminding and redirecting.

another area and settle down without help. Chasing and rolling trucks into the center space were also noticeable problems during most self-selection and cleanup periods. As soon as children entered that empty middle space, their behavior seemed to change. In response, the teacher's behavior changed too, from cheerful support of learning activity to correcting and restraining their behavior.

Classroom Space and Behavior

The study of physical space by Kritchevsky and Prescott developed several concepts and principles to identify and describe relationships between spatial organization and behavior in young children's environments. Those principles offer a useful tool for planning and organizing space in learning environments for older children as well. Central concepts in the study are *units,* the spaces arranged for children's activity; *surrounding space,* the space around a unit needed for movement by people using it; and *paths,* spaces used to move through the environment. They are the basis for the discussions of spatial organization presented in this chapter.[1]

The environment-behavior relationships shown in Kritchevsky and Prescott's work describe how teacher-arranged spaces, created with furniture arrangement, encourage children to act in ways that may or may not have been intended by the teacher. Strong spatial messages urge children to move in this direction or that, to enter or leave an area, to pause and read or pass by without attending. Space invites children to talk with others, hurry or move calmly, touch others or leave them alone, combine materials or keep them separated. When the resulting behavior is unexpected or unwanted, teachers tend to recite rules, redirect, scold, or restrain children. On the other hand, when behavior encouraged by the environment is expected and desired, teachers are more likely to respond in positive ways that support activities and learning. In either situation, spatial organization is a strong influence on both teacher and child behavior.

The environment can facilitate movement useful for working and learning when spatial organization and the teacher's interactions encourage the same behaviors. Movement is a normal accompaniment to learning experiences for children. Individuals move about in purposeful ways that contribute to their work. They share ideas and work activity as

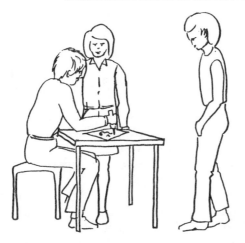

Movement helps children contact one another and share ideas.

their movements put them in contact with others at work. Movement provides communication as children pass and scan displays of information and materials, or the products of other children's study.

When spatial organization encourages movements and other behaviors that conflict with the teacher's wishes, the potential productivity and communication of classroom movement is lost. The conflicting suggestions stimulate disruptive behavior that can also puzzle teachers. It's easy to assume that the problem lies with the children, but the teacher-arranged environment is really at fault. Because environmental messages are strong, teachers can unknowingly encourage children to act quite differently from the ways the teachers expect by the arrangement of classroom furniture. When this happens, much energy and time must be spent verbally setting and enforcing behavior expectations that contradict the behavior suggestions made inadvertently through spatial organization

Places for Activity

When teachers arrange classroom furniture, one of their first concerns is to provide places for children's activity. There are many different kinds of learning activities in most environments, so the *units* in which those activities occur must also vary in size, shape, location, and provisioning. Potential units, several kinds of activity units, and undesignated units all offer space for children's activity.

Potential Units

A defined space in the environment that hasn't been provisioned for children's activity is a *potential unit*. It consists of empty space surrounded by visible or tangible boundaries.[2] An empty table can be a potential unit: its edges form boundaries that are tangible and visible, while the empty space of the surface invites children to settle down beside it. Some potential units are formed by furniture arrangements placing large furniture pieces at right angles to each other, creating tangible boundaries on two sides with a visual but intangible boundary on a third. The clear, empty space of a potential unit invites children to go to that space for their activity.

A standing teacher who looks over the environment tends to see teacher-planned potential units like table surfaces or floor spaces with physical boundaries. But potential units also exist in unplanned places. Corner floor spaces behind opened doors make inviting potential units. The door, the walls meeting in the corner, and an implied line across the opened side of the space form boundaries. In other places opened doorways may invite children into empty closets or into the space between opened doors of a cabinet. Carpet edging, the structural space beneath a stairway, floor space under a primary table, or a rectangle of light shining through a window onto the floor can all define potential units. Sometimes children see and receive invitations from potential units that have been overlooked by teachers, and their resulting behavior may be puzzling to adults.

[2]*Ibid., p. 9.*

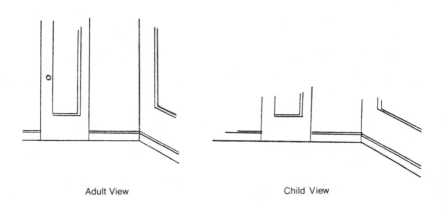

Adult View   Child View

Children can receive messages from potential units overlooked by teachers.

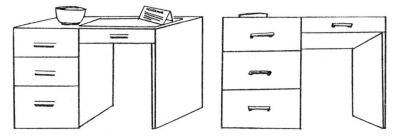

A teacher's desk looks different to children than to adults.

Adults may see plenty of table space for children to use for working places in the environment, but small children may see the spaces beneath the tables more clearly than their surfaces. The important parts of the teacher's desk are clear from adult height: the desk top and the drawers. But from a lower view, different features become dominant, and the space designed as a kneehole may be very inviting.

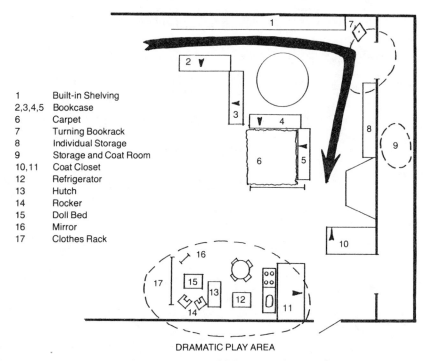

1	Built-in Shelving
2,3,4,5	Bookcase
6	Carpet
7	Turning Bookrack
8	Individual Storage
9	Storage and Coat Room
10,11	Coat Closet
12	Refrigerator
13	Hutch
14	Rocker
15	Doll Bed
16	Mirror
17	Clothes Rack

DRAMATIC PLAY AREA

The traffic pattern took children past the open door.

Making Use of Potential Units

A kindergarten teacher in a converted elementary classroom wondered why the children left the main part of the classroom so often to run into the empty coat room. They teased, chased, peeked out the door, and called to the other children. Then she saw that the traffic pattern in the room took children past the door of the coat room and that the empty space offered strong invitations.

There were several ways the teacher could reorganize space to encourage different behaviors by the children. She could remove the potential unit by arranging different traffic patterns so the children wouldn't pass the inviting potential unit so often, or she could block the doorway with a piece of furniture. But she decided to take advantage of the additional space the potential unit offered by adding materials and equipment for the children's activity. She divided the coat room with a screen across the middle. Half the space became part of the dramatic play area, furnished with kitchen equipment and props, while the rest of the area's equipment was arranged outside but near the doorway. Now, when children entered the old coat room, most of their activity was guided by the materials available in the unit. The teacher also gained some additional storage space in the rest of the coat room, which no longer functioned as a potential unit because it wasn't empty.

When children are observed in some puzzling behavior, check the environment for overlooked potential units. Looking around from children's eye level and from different places may reveal inviting spaces not

The coat room was equipped with house equipment.

visible from adult eye level. If the behaviors generated by the potential unit seem inappropriate, the unit can be removed or provisioned, and children's behavior will begin to change. Turning furniture around so openings are less visible, rerouting traffic, or covering openings are all ways to eliminate potential units. Equipping the potential unit with particular materials for children's use influences their behavior there, as the material will suggest some activities rather than others. Provisioning the previously overlooked potential units encourages children to work in spaces that they have already found inviting and comfortable. This in effect adds available space to the learning environment without a major reorganization.

Although unrecognized potential units can sometimes generate unexpected behaviors, planned potential units can offer considerable flexibility in the environment. They can be used by individuals or small groups who bring provisions to the unit, and they are available for special-interest, short-term arrangements that don't require a permanently provisioned unit. A wheeled wardrobe forms a potential unit during seasons when it isn't needed for outdoor clothing; cushions soften the space while books, pictures, and a tape recorder provision the unit. When a lighted storage closet kept attracting children in an elementary classroom, the teacher reorganized higher levels for put-away storage, then added a small table, books and pictures, and a variety of consumable materials for children's use.

Similarly, the linoleum edge near some built-in cabinets in an elementary classroom seemed to call attention to a potential unit on the

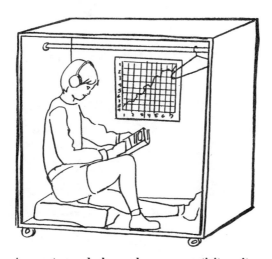

An empty wardrobe can become an activity unit.

A lighted storage closet can be provisioned for activity.

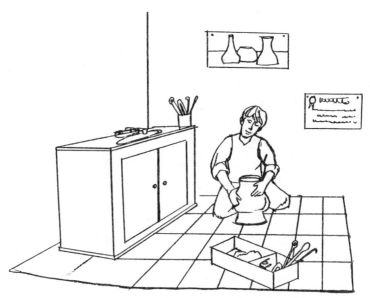

The linoleum defined a potential unit, so the teacher provisioned it.

**The space under the bookrack was equipped with
a tape recorder and earphones.**

floor, which was often occupied by children. The teacher equipped the space with materials and tools for sculpture, and a caddy of common tools and materials. Information about the care of tools and pictures of sculpture were displayed on the lower part of the wall nearby. And when the space beneath a sandwich-board bookrack proved attractive to some third graders, it became a good activity unit for one person when a tape recorder with earphones, tapes, and some common tools and materials were added.

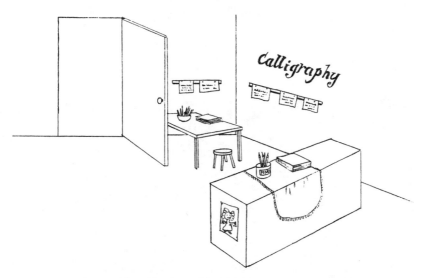

When equipped, a potential unit becomes an activity unit.

A potential unit behind a closet door can become a sheltered place for one person when a low, small table with materials and tools for an activity such as calligraphy is added. Low tack strips on the wall near the table invite display of work and samples of lettering.

Activity Units

When the kindergarten teacher of the classroom shown on page 53 (bottom) equipped the empty space of an inviting coat room, she arranged an *activity unit*—a unit containing something for children to use.[3] There are several different kinds of activity units, serving somewhat different purposes.

Some activity units are provisioned with special materials or equipment to designate particular kinds of activity. Construction areas and painting places are examples of this type. So are units provisioned for experimenting, exploring natural materials, and making music. Other activity units, provisioned only with a basic assortment of common tools and materials, are left undesignated, and can support many different activities during the course of the day. These undesignated units differ from potential units, since they have general provisions to support the activity of children who enter the unit with a purpose in mind.

Activity units can also be described in terms of the amount of seclusion they offer. Elizabeth Jones has suggested three ways of arrang-

[3]*Ibid., p. 11.*

Some activity units are provisioned to designate kinds of activity.

A low table offers several possible uses within a unit.

ing activity units so that children don't always have to function as members of a large group. Corners, or other spaces with one or two-sided protection, offer some shelter as *partially screened units. Insulated units* are small areas with three-sided protection for three or four people, while *individual hide units* provide smaller, close spaces where one or two children can feel complete privacy.[4] The seclusion provided in these units is arranged by furniture defining the units, rather than by their distance from other areas.

The amount of space arranged in a particular unit, and the extent to which shelter is needed, often depend on the provisions of the unit and the activities they suggest. A low table offers a variety of uses with a partially screened unit. Many children are comfortable sitting on floor cushions as they finish written work at the table. At other times the table is a good height for construction or other projects. A table within an insulated unit can be used with a variety of equipment. When needed, floor cushions offer seating. The table and chairs are also available for individual seating.

A table beside a path offers a good stopping place to sit with a book, jot down notes, or use information from charts hung on a standing divider. At other times the table can offer seating for two or three children for special, everybody-seated activities. Dividers or revolving bookcases can define the path and offer partial screening to children working at the table.

---

[4]*Elizabeth Jones*, Dimensions of Teaching-Learning Environments: Handbook for Teachers *(Pasadena: Pacific Oaks College Bookstore, 1973), pp. 14–15.*

The table in an insulated unit is used with a variety of equipment.

A table beside a path offers a good stopping place.

Space for Movement

Some activity units have clearly visible edges that seem to contain the activity of the children working there. Walls, furniture, shelving, or other tangible boundaries define sufficient space for children's activity. In other units, however, children move across or through the space of the unit itself and also through the space surrounding it.

Surrounding Space

A unit in use requires the space occupied by its equipment or provisions, and also some empty *surrounding space* for movement. When children use an activity unit made of a provisioned table with

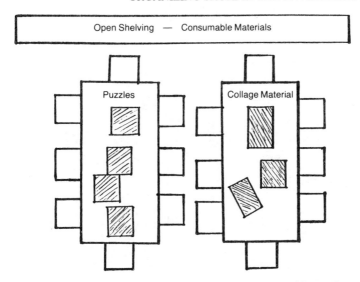

The teacher thought there was enough space to use either unit.

chairs and a storage shelf, they use quite a bit of surrounding space as they work. They may stand up to reach across the table, push chairs all the way back to rise and walk to the shelf, walk behind occupied chairs, or stand beside the table to watch others.[5]

A teacher who tried to organize two activity units beside the same storage cabinet (as shown in figure above) thought there was enough space for children to use either unit comfortably. One table was provisioned with puzzles, the other with materials for making collage. The teacher expected children at each unit to use the materials on the table, and perhaps additional items from the nearby shelves. Each table with its chairs and materials was meant to be a separate activity unit.

When the children began to use the units, however, the space appeared quite different. Chairs from one table were pushed back, bumping children at the other table. People moving to the shelves tried to squeeze between the tables and so added to the crowding. Children complained about interference, materials fell to the floor, and cardboard puzzle pieces got glued into the collages. Obviously, although the teacher thought the arrangement left ample space between the tables, there really wasn't enough. Children in each of the units used surrounding space as well as furniture space. Surrounding space is difficult to see until children actually begin to use activity units, because its boundaries usually aren't tangible. However, it is an important part of an activity unit and is not really available for other uses.

[5]*Kritchevsky, Prescott, and Walling,* Planning Environments, *p. 11.*

People tried to squeeze between the tables.

When the surrounding space of two units overlaps, several results are predictable. Physical interference like bumping, jostling, and knocking materials off tables or out of hands is unintended but frequent. Many complaints, and sometimes arguments, follow. There is considerable interruption for children in either unit who become involved or are distracted by events in the other unit. Children in the overlapping units will seem to have short attention spans, but in other settings they may show more sustained involvement.

Overlapping surrounding space often causes children using two units to perceive them as one space. It's natural for them to combine materials they perceive as being in the same space, because the placement of materials side by side suggests their combination. Although it seems clear to any adult that puzzle pieces glued into collage result in unusable puzzles, spatial organization encourages children to combine them. The suggestion of the spatial organization can be much stronger than rules or adult views of common sense.

Paths

Spatial arrangement can cause *paths* to intrude into surrounding space. This creates problems for children working in the unit, much like those of overlapping surrounding space. Spatial organization functions best when there is enough surrounding space for the movement involved in the use of units, and when paths are clear and empty.[6]

[6]*Ibid, p. 23.*

A clear path is a visible, broad, empty space that seems to be going somewhere, with something interesting at the end of it. The path tends to draw people from one place to another and facilitates movement of children through the environment. To function well, the space arranged for paths should not be available for other uses.[7]

Sometimes teachers see paths clearly but are puzzled because children aren't using them. Some paths seen from teacher height just disappear at the working level of the children. Furniture can completely block the children's view of a path, without interfering at all with the teacher's overview. Since the purpose of spatial organization is to facilitate the activity and movement of the children, it is necessary to find out what children see from their chair or floor-level work spaces, and from their standing and walking eye levels, too. Teacher-planned paths that aren't seen by children aren't really paths at all.

In a classroom with the desks arranged in a T-shape, as shown below, the teacher was puzzled at the children's apparent disinterest in the invitingly displayed materials of an activity unit behind the desk group, whereas activity units to the left and right of it were well used. As she talked about the arrangement to a colleague, they looked across from

[7]*Ibid., p. 18.*

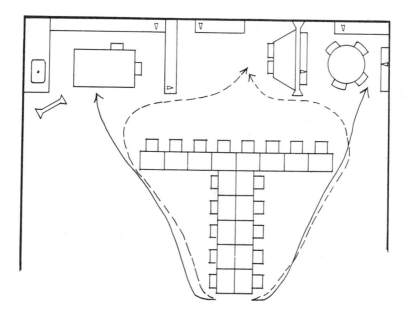

The teacher's clear paths were invisible from the children's eye level.

the end of the desk group to the activity units. Both teachers saw paths that were broad, empty and clear. Only when they tested the paths by moving along them, stopping to look ahead from children's eye level, did they understand that both paths disappeared about halfway along their length, where different paths, unseen from adult height, drew children to the activity units on the right or left. For the children the back row of desks, extending out to the sides of the large T-arrangement, concealed the opening into the unused unit and highlighted the activity units beside it.

There are other reasons, too, why some activity units provisioned with interesting materials receive little use. When the path to such a unit enters the surrounding space of another unit, a child moving toward the first unit must pass through this different unit on the way, where friends, events, or materials are also interesting. The child may become involved with the people or activities, or with problem solving about space-created conflicts, and forget the original destination.

Sometimes, in an environment with many well-provisioned areas, some activity units seem to receive almost constant use, generating strong competition among large numbers of children all attracted to the unit at the same time. Some children tend to gather almost exclusively at

Some children go to the nearest unit and don't encounter others.

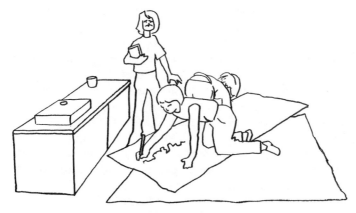

When activities expand into paths, there is interference.

one activity unit, although materials and resources of other units have high interest potential. Checking children's views of paths and observing traffic patterns often show that the much-used activity units are located near the beginning of a path, close to the place where everybody moves out into the environment. The provisions of the high-use units are usually appealing, and children are quickly attracted into the area. Once involved with the materials and activities within the unit, they don't move on through the environment to encounter other possibilities. Choice patterns often expand when the popular unit is relocated so that interested children still have access to it; the new paths that take them there can help children encounter other activity units along the way.

When activities expand from activity units into the space intended for paths, interference results. Special problems arise when murals, block constructions, or other projects on the floor intrude into paths, especially for younger children. From their height, small children can't see as large an area of space at one time as adults can. To the moving child, who is looking ahead to the activity unit he is eager to reach, a block construction or mural on the floor may not be visible. The intruder may be as surprised as the painters are to find himself suddenly walking on a mural.[8]

Dead Space

Sometimes clear paths draw children into empty space that is too large to be clearly defined as a unit. When such a large, empty space is located near the center of the environment, with strong paths leading in but not out, it often functions as *dead space*.[9] When children are drawn

[8]*Ibid, p. 18.*
[9]*Ibid, p. 19.*

into dead space, they tend to stay in it, because there aren't clear paths to lead them out. Since the space is empty of materials to influence or focus activity, dead space tends to generate a boisterous, loose socialization or disorganized physical movement. In older children this takes the form of teasing, roughhousing, mock fighting, or some flirting; younger children resort to disorganized running, chasing, roughhousing, and sliding.

The kindergarten teacher whose environment was described at the beginning of the chapter had trouble starting the day with the children because of dead space in the middle of the environment. Once in the center, children were surrounded by empty space with a lot of unfocused furniture around the edges. The effects of the dead space were stronger than the children's and the teacher's best intentions.

When dead space appears in classrooms for young children, it usually results from placement of activity units along the walls. Empty space in the center is often planned for large group activities and for traffic. Placing a line of unprovisioned tables in a large dead space is more apt to provide something to run around than to define the space. It is best improved by reconsidering spatial organization of most of the environment, and establishing clear paths to defined units and spaces.

It is not easy to create dead space in classrooms for older children, because larger furniture and children leave less total empty space, but it

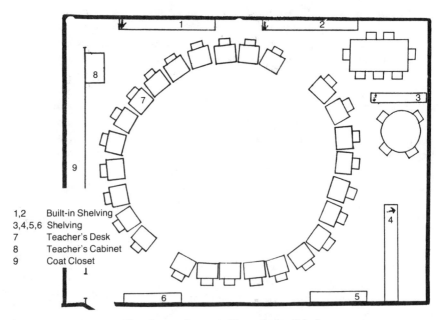

1,2   Built-in Shelving
3,4,5,6 Shelving
7   Teacher's Desk
8   Teacher's Cabinet
9   Coat Closet

Dead space is created by a circle of desks.

is possible. When dead space appears in these classrooms, it is usually created by desks or tables arranged in a large circle or hollow square, so that students are facing one another. Children may enter the center area through open spaces intended to provide a path across the area, then find themselves in dead space. When children gather in the center area, it takes a good deal of reminding and redirecting to move them out of it and into other areas of the environment. The space in the center of the seating arrangement can be changed by equipping it with some furniture and provisioning it for small group activity. A shelf unit or low divider can define a path and help children move through the center space rather than being caught in it.

Defining Spaces in the Environment

Spaces intended for special purposes can be visually defined in several ways within the environment. Placing the backs of larger furniture pieces toward paths helps set off activity units from the paths clearly. Dividers placed at the edges of surrounding space can define and separate spaces intended for sustained activity. When furniture color contrasts with wall color, the increased visibility of the furniture can call attention to the activity units and define more clearly the edges of paths.

Sometimes a change in levels created by a low platform of wood, an extra bookcase lying on its face, or a layer of masonry or wooden blocks,

Sometimes a change in levels can define a working place.

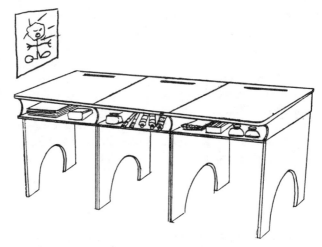

Extra flat-topped desks can serve as dividers and shelving.

can define a working space. Extra flat-topped desks can serve as dividers while at the same time providing shelving or working places. They offer several ways to define space because they can be arranged in different patterns. Low dividers can define the edges of surrounding space for a special unit. The dividers don't interfere with the visibility of paths because children easily see over them.

Pillars made from long carpet tubing anchored in plaster of Paris, can divide space and at the same time offer display possibilities. Shelv-

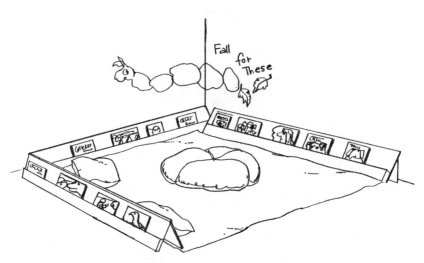

Very low dividers can define edges of a unit.

Pillars divide space and offer display.

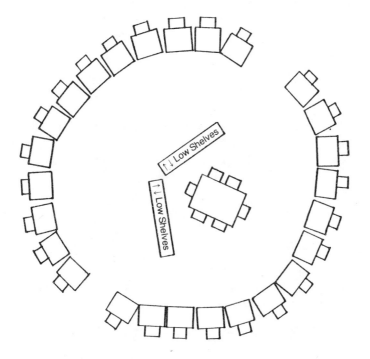

Furniture can change dead space into an activity unit and define a path.

Furniture backs separate space for units from paths.

ing, tables, materials, and chairs can turn empty central spaces into places for learning activities, and also define a path through the center of the environment. Furniture backs offer a good separation between activity units and paths, and with fabric backing can also display useful information.

Checking Your Own Environment

Does the spatial organization of your learning environment facilitate the activity and movements of children in their work? You can check this by observing the paths children use, the amount of interference they experience, and their movement through the environment. This can be done in two fifteen-minute observation periods. During one period you'll watch an individual child, and during the other you'll observe a particular area of the environment. Movements can be recorded on a sketch map of your environment.

1. Prepare a sketch map of your learning environment. Draw a rough sketch of the room, furniture placement, and built-in features. Two copies will be helpful, so information from each observation can be recorded on a separate copy.
2. Select one child as a focus for observation. During a ten or fifteen-minute period, observe and record the child's movement and actions, especially:
   — where the child locates for work
   — where the child travels for materials

— what traffic routes are used
— how often the child moves from one place to another
— how many people interact with or interrupt the child
Record the child's movements through the environment on the sketch map. Record also the place and number of interactions with other people.

3. Select one place as the focal point for the next observation, preferably a place where one person is working. Observe and record all movement in and around the focal point, noting especially:
— where the traffic passes or approaches that space
— the number of people who enter the surrounding space of the area
— the frequency with which children interact in the area
— any episodes of physical contact
— any instances of conflict (polite or otherwise)
Record the observed information on the sketch map.

4. Review the information recorded on your sketch maps for the following information:
— any surrounding spaces that overlap
— indications of dead space at the center of things
— unclarified traffic routes
— crowded paths
— areas with high levels of distraction

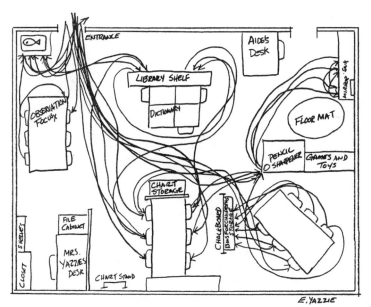

Record of traffic in Mrs. Yazzie's classroom.

— teacher-designed traffic routes used by children
— children's own traffic routes not designed by teacher

If you have recorded children walking from one place to another, you may be startled at the density of traffic in certain areas. Many teachers find that unless they actually look at the records of events, they have only a vague perception of where movement takes place. Your sketch maps may show you some needed changes or additions to spatial organization, even though the arrangement worked well several weeks ago. Events, activities, and children change from month to month in any learning environment, and spatial organization often needs to change, too.

SECTION II

PROVISIONING FOR LEARNING

CHAPTER 4

A BASIC FRAMEWORK FOR PROVISIONING

Keeping the environment provisioned with the necessary equipment, supplies, and information to support learning is a constant occupation for teachers. Provisions play several different roles in learning experiences. They shape the activity and its content and enable children to sustain productive activity without continuous teacher direction. Children's ability to initiate and carry out appropriate experiences depends upon the extent that six basic categories of provisioning are represented in the environment. Each category affects learning activities in certain ways. Equipment and materials from all categories provide the basic framework for provisioning needed to stimulate and support activities and explorations of learners.

Which Provisions?

Several teachers at the new elementary school were complaining to one another about what was going on in their learning environments. They were annoyed at both the children and themselves. Behavior became disruptive as soon as a few children finished their assignments. Children wandered about and pestered one another, noise levels rose, materials were handled carelessly and with little interest. By late morning it was almost impossible for a teacher to give full attention to the children in a reading group, because so many of the other children also required attention. The teachers even had to put materials into some children's hands so they would have something to do, which took more time and attention from the teaching groups.

Most of the teachers weren't willing to think that it was entirely the children's problem. They saw enough different behaviors during group work to know the students could be quite serious about their studies. Most of the children were persistent about working on assignments, except when they were interrupted too often by wanderers.

Everybody at the school had spent a lot of time before the school year began, getting the environments ready for children. The teachers had chosen equipment, ordered supplies, made instructional materials, assembled a library, prepared learning centers. They thought the environments were well provisioned and should have given children plenty of useful things to do when their assignments were finished. But the children weren't finding appropriate things to do. There was little long-term involvement and self-direction.

While they tried to identify what problems in the learning environment might contribute to students' lack of self-direction, the teachers reviewed the checklist used when they first provisioned the classrooms. With the help of the checklist, each environment had been stocked with plenty of texts, math materials, seating furniture, games, writing paper, maps, scissors, dictionaries, and other items. According to the provisioning framework the teachers had used, each environment was adequately provisioned to support children's involvement in both teacher-directed and self-directed learning activities. The involvement in teacher-directed activities was fine, but the self-directed learning activities weren't happening.

The faculty tried an experiment. They separated into small groups, and each group went into a learning environment. There they tried to find something to do and then stay with that activity for at least one half-hour. The teachers were surprised to find that they didn't do this any better than the children, for there was little to interest them. There were teacher-prepared games and activities available, but they were all for a specific grade level or instructional purpose and didn't offer activity possibilities outside the lesson setting. Supplementary books, math materials, puzzles, word-matching kits, and map-reading exercises also failed to hold their attention. The teachers handled a few materials, leafed through some books, and gazed at a map or two, but basically their activity was social as they chatted with one another.

Later, discussing their experiences, they compared their difficulty in finding something to do with the children's problems. They remembered that children's unfocused behaviors occurred when quite a few of them had finished with their teacher-directed assignments. Like the teachers in the same environments, these children couldn't find something to do. The available equipment and materials didn't offer enough possibilities for self-directed learning activities.

The teachers began to think that their checklist, with long lists of texts, specific instructional materials, and learning games, wasn't very useful for provisioning an environment to support continuous learning outside of lessons and assignments. Of course they could always assume that each learning environment would be provisioned with texts, kits, and other instructional materials selected for every grade level in the school district. District-wide materials lists were used to guide the making of special materials and teaching games to supplement the commercial materials. Provisioning for direct instruction could be done without a checklist, but a guide to provisioning for children's self-directed involvement in learning was badly needed. What provisions were essential?

The teachers returned to the classrooms again. This time they compared the environments where teachers described severe problems of involvement and self-direction with those where children were better able to sustain learning activity. They saw that each environment was provisioned differently, and tried to identify the consistent characteristics of provisioning in those that were more supportive.

After several days and many brainstorming sessions, the teachers agreed on a basic list of essentials, beyond the assigned and supplementary instructional materials, that were necessary for children to independently find learning activities. They identified six:

Raw materials: materials that can be used to make products, to record and preserve information, to transmit ideas and messages, to experiment.

Tools: objects and equipment used to do something to the materials and information as students create products and messages, conduct experiments, and explore information and ideas.

Information sources: specific information and facts about many different topics to be investigated, observed, studied, and communicated to others.

Containers: something to hold materials, projects, or information during activities, or to preserve them for later use.

Work spaces: empty places where students can find room to work with materials and equipment.

Display facilities: places and materials for students to exhibit their own work and communications.

The teachers now had a new checklist to use as they reviewed each learning environment, predicting its capacity to sustain involvement and provide stimulus and support for self-directed learning activity. Instead of lengthy lists of specific classroom supplies and texts, they had a basic framework for provisioning consisting of just six categories.[1]

The teachers applied their checklist of *raw materials, tools, information sources, containers, work spaces,* and *display facilities* to provisioning throughout the school year. They used the checklist again for setting up the learning environment at the beginning of the following year, and were able to identify many specific supplies and materials that might serve each category of the checklist. This meant that they were free to choose among specific items, as long as all categories were adequately represented. They found that environments supported sustained involvement in both teacher-directed and self-directed learning when the specialized instructional materials matched the instructional levels of the specific children, and when the functions represented by each provisioning category were well represented.

Six Categories for Provisioning

The teachers who developed the checklist for provisioning found a framework that helped them look at the environment's potential support for children's continuous involvement with learning activities. They discovered that environments were usually well provisioned for teacher-directed instructional activities, but the teachers also needed a way to look at a broader base of provisioning. They wanted a tool to tell them when the environment could support independent activities related to the instructional sessions. They needed to know when an environment was ready to engage children's interest in self-initiated learning, and whether it offered appropriate provisions to sustain the activities and investigations generated by that interest. The teachers found that when all those conditions were met, they could be reasonably sure that children could find and develop interesting things to do and that their activities would be productive for learning. Changes in the learning environment throughout the year, as it responded to children's changing learning needs, could occur within the same framework.

The teachers' framework for basic provisioning works well because it identifies a group of essential functions that are necessary for provisioning to support continuous learning. It isn't necessary to inventory all the materials in the learning environment to judge its adequacy. A teacher can check for the presence of an assortment of provisions within the framework of the six categories of *raw materials, tools, information sources, containers, work spaces,* and *display facilities.* When the functions of each category are well represented in the environmental provisions, potential support for children's involvement in learning is strong.

Raw Materials for Many Activities

In their learning experiences children manipulate, shape, arrange, combine, and recombine a variety of raw materials. Consumable raw materials such as paint, paper, or clay must be replaced, but permanent raw materials like blocks can be reused. There are as many uses for raw materials as there are children in the learning environment, and the variety of potentially useful raw materials is extensive. Natural materials, construction materials, found items, pigments, papers, foods, cords, fabrics, and sculpture materials can all contribute to the complexity and diversity of learning activities. The specific materials that serve as raw materials range from stationery, styrofoam, and spools to food coloring, feathers, yarn, and drawing paper.

Different Kinds of Raw Materials

Permanent and consumable *construction materials* support a variety of projects. Solid and skeletal construction materials offer different possibilities, and a variety of scales from toothpick size to pieces of lumber are useful.

Some *natural materials* lend themselves to creative projects and exploration activities. *Found items* once served a purpose in some manufactured product; their original functions and their forms add to the interest they hold for children. Various *fabrics* and *cords* can be draped,

Construction materials on different scales support varied activities.

Natural materials and found objects are used in creative projects.

Fabrics and cords can be draped, cut, joined, or worn.

Different papers hold words or images and make things.

Pigments can be used for experimentation and practical crafts.

cut, joined, or worn as a part of children's learning activity. *Papers* with different surfaces, textures, shapes, colors, and consistency serve almost every learning activity in some way. Papers receive words or images, are shaped into new forms and structures, and decorate objects and spaces.

Pigments lend themselves very well to experimentation, practical crafts, and expressive activities. Children learn a lot by testing dyes from natural materials, by matching shade and intensity of paints, and by observing the movement of food coloring through liquids. *Foods* serve a number of purposes in learning activities. In addition to cooking, or feeding classroom animals, they can be used in collage, in experimentation and exploration of physical properties, and as dramatic props.

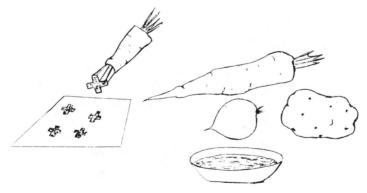

Foods can play many roles in learning activities.

Sculpture materials can be shaped and molded.

Sculpture materials are useful for model making, a variety of creative projects, or exploring texture and malleability.

Contributions of Raw Materials

Children use quantities of raw materials in their learning activities. Consumables need frequent replacement, and reusable materials receive almost constant use. Fortunately, raw materials are often available through recycling of scrap materials from the community, and these sources add to catalogue-ordered supplies in interesting ways.

Although the quantity of raw materials directly available to learners is important, variety is essential to stimulate and support different kinds of learning activities. Replacing part of any large supply of a single raw material, such as manila drawing paper, with smaller amounts of different materials from the same group like cardboard, wallpaper, tissue, printer's scraps, and shelf paper, will change the activity possibilities. Sometimes a rearrangement of raw materials can be as effective as increasing the amount and variety, since materials appear different in different surroundings.

Tools for a Variety of Functions

The objects and equipment that children can use to process materials or information are called tools. This category of the provisioning checklist includes a good many items not ordinarily labeled tools, but which are used to act upon information or materials. Several specific functions are served by tools: computing, measuring, recording, joining, cutting and shaping, mixing, viewing, expressing and communicating and heating and cooling. The objects and materials useful as tools are as diverse as paste, calculators, hammers, egg beaters, telephones, crayons, tape measures, and magnifying glasses.

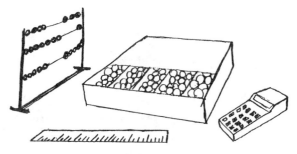

Computing tools help children process data.

Different Kinds of Tools

Computing tools help children process information in many different ways. Possibilities include simple everyday items, as well as more sophisticated equipment. *Tools for measuring* are used on time, weight, volume, and dimensions of solid forms and surfaces. Calibrated tools are important, but many uncalibrated units of measure are equally useful. Recording events, information, and ideas can be done in many ways: a variety of *recording tools* permits children at all levels of skill development to preserve and communicate their findings and experiences.

Joining tools are needed for many activities; some tools join materials permanently, while others hold objects in place. Some *cutting and shaping tools* can be used fairly casually, but others require careful placement, ample work space, and clear instructions for safe and successful use. Children use *mixing tools* for pigments, recipe ingredients, assorted solutions, and soft sculpture materials.

Measuring tools are used for time, weight, and volume.

**Recording tools help children of many skill levels
to preserve information.**

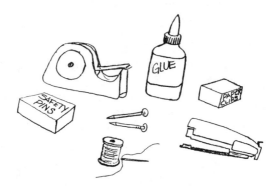

Joining tools are needed for many activities.

Some cutting tools can be used casually, but others require caution.

Pigments, batters, and other mixtures require mixing tools.

Tools for viewing are used to obtain information from many sources that display data. Some viewing tools make difficult-to-see things more visible, and others hold specimens so they can be observed. *Expressing and communicating tools* let children share their creative activities with others and communicate information about events and ideas. As children explore and experiment with materials, *tools for heating and cooling* can maintain or alter the temperature of those materials.

Contributions of Tools

Tools are in great demand and need to be available for almost every learning activity in the environment. Because of this, both the number and the distribution of tools are important, and so is the variety of tools available for use. A collection of different tools for any function, such as a hem gauge, trundle wheel, tape measure, and folding rule for linear measurement, supports more activities than a collection of duplicates like a bundle of one-foot wooden rulers, all calibrated to the quarter-inch. No specific tools are as essential in the environment as the presence of some tools, preferably a variety, for each important function served. by tools. Variety can be provided in several ways and can cost less than

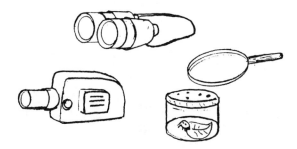

Viewing tools are used to get information from many sources.

Tools for expression help children communicate with others.

duplicating the same tools. Many tools are common objects: some can be contributed from households and other community sources, and some may be borrowed or shared with another environment.

Information for Learning

Information sources offer a range of data, in print and nonprint forms, about the numerous topics and subject areas that reflect the planned content of the curriculum and the content of children's interests. Some, such as animals and posters, display their information so that it can be obtained by looking at the information source. Others, like phonograph records and picture files, contain stored information. Information sources can be references, recordings, media, labels, natural

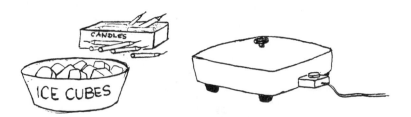

Tools for heating and cooling support experimentation and exploration.

References and recordings store information.

specimens, living things, realia, charts, pictures, or books. The specific items that serve as information sources are as varied as newspapers, soil samples, package directions, encyclopedias, seedlings, almanacs, and blueprints.

Different Kinds of Information Sources

Catalogues, phone books, and word lists as well as more conventional *references* offer specific information to students. *Recordings*, made with specialized equipment, also store information for later re-

Media and labels are familiar sources of information.

**Natural specimens and living things offer variable
and unpredictable information.**

Models and realia represent the real world.

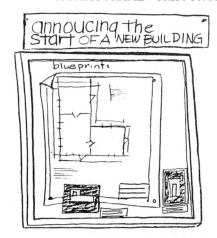

Charts and pictures carry information across their faces.

trieval. Familiar forms of communication *media* offer a breadth of information. *Labels* offer another familiar form of information with details that are sometimes overlooked. *Natural specimens* of inanimate or once-living things yield a good deal of information through examination. *Living things,* observed over time, can offer information that is variable and sometimes unpredictable.

The information offered by *models* depends on the accuracy with which they represent their subjects. *Realia* seem to hold great interest as information sources, since they are samples of objects from the real world. Maps, blueprints, and other forms of *charts* carry their information across their faces. *Pictures,* often on a smaller scale, also carry information across the face. Trade books, appliance manuals, song books, and teachers' editions are a few kinds of *books* that can extend the information available.

Tradebooks, appliance manuals, and other books offer valuable information.

Contributions of Information Sources

The amount of actual information in the environment is more important that the number of information sources, because a lot of information is required to keep students involved in learning, and information used in learning covers many topics. Because the second or fifteenth copy of the same dictionary or any other information source brings no additional information, duplicating information sources doesn't extend the knowledge resources of the environment.

Within every group of learners, individuals differ in skill development. Different children approach the task of obtaining information differently and may use a given information source in different ways. A learning environment offers the best support for learning activities when there is at least one print or nonprint information source available to each child on many different topics, so the child can gather information independently, regardless of the level of skill development. To help children pursue topics further, some information sources that display data can be combined with those that store more detailed information. Information sources illustrate the many different ways there are to search, obtain, and store information. Different kinds of information sources require different skills, so they also stimulate a range of skills as children gather information.

Many information sources are purchased within the restrictions of school budgets, but additional sources are usually needed. In most communities public, private, and business organizations can contribute many, and borrowing is sometimes helpful. Special globes, maps, library books, and references can be shared within a school. These can extend the information of the environment, even though they aren't permanently located there.

Containers for Storing and Arranging

Children use containers to store information materials and work in progress, or to arrange and organize information and materials during a learning activity. Since a variety of materials and forms of information are used by children in the course of a day, many different kinds of containers are useful. Flats, deep containers, watertight containers, racks, envelopes, chart papers, and blank books are included in this category. The specific objects that serve as containers range from trays, graph paper, and medicine vials to paper sacks, cigar boxes, and photo albums.

Different Kinds of Containers

Trays, box lids, and meat trays are a few of the *flats* that students can use to organize and store materials. Like flats, *deep containers* such

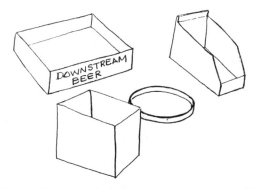

Flats and deep containers organize and store materials.

as bins, tool caddies, and shoe boxes aren't necessarily watertight. *Watertight containers* hold liquids and are often useful to children as they prepare materials they will use in their learning activities. *Racks* are useful for holding large, flat materials so they don't have to be folded or crumpled. On a smaller scale, *envelopes* are useful for flat objects, too, and also hold other small objects.

Graph paper, posterboard, and other specialized *chart papers* are helpful for organizing or holding specific data as it is gathered, or for later use in the learning activity. *Blank books* such as scrapbooks and ledgers can serve a similar purpose, or be used for long-term storage of collected information.

Contributions of Containers

The sizes and characteristics of children's learning materials and projects, and the forms of information gathered, help determine which

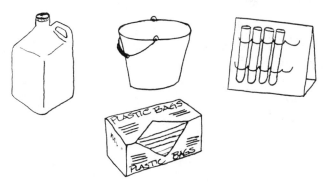

Watertight containers are useful for preparing materials.

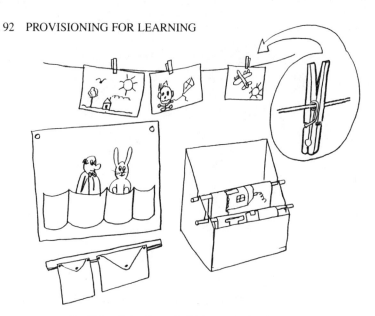

Racks and envelopes hold flat and odd-shaped objects.

BIRTHDAY CHART			
January			
February			
March			
April			
May			
June			
July			
August			
September			
October			
November			
December			

Chart papers and blank books can store collected information.

objects in the environment are needed as containers. Shape, storage capacity, size, and adaptability are also important. Since many potential containers could easily serve different purposes in the learning environment, children may need help in distinguishing between containers and similar objects intended for other purposes. Egg cartons, for instance, make good containers and also good raw materials, while a large beaker may be designated as either a container or a volume-measuring tool. Containers can be identified by their location in the environment, by the surrounding materials, or through labeling.

Individual and Group Work Spaces

Work spaces provide the places where children can work in the learning environment. Some work spaces were described as potential units and activity units in Chapter Three, but there are also other ways to identify the many kinds of places that can be arranged for children and their learning materials. Most of the time work spaces are occupied by individuals or groups of children with their materials, but sometimes work spaces are just surfaces to hold materials as children settle alongside. It's common to think of work spaces as horizontal surfaces like table tops, but booths, corners, mats, "underneath" areas, and vertical surfaces also provide space for learning activities. The specific work spaces developed within those groups range from counter tops and easels to rug samples and carrels.

Different Kinds of Work Spaces

Folding screens, table dividers, and other enclosing arrangements can create *booths,* so individuals can work alone and be undisturbed. *Corners* provide work spaces for small groups or individuals. Several different kinds of *mats* offer portable work spaces that can be used to spread out materials or to provide floor seating. Many children are comfortable in *underneath* work spaces; spaces beneath tables, a loft, or a simple canopy offer shelter from intrusion. But some learning activities and materials demand a firm surface. A variety of *vertical surfaces* can be arranged to hold paper for chart making or creative work, while *horizontal surfaces* can be found or created in many locations.

Contributions of Work Spaces

There are many ways to organize work spaces near materials storage, so children have materials at hand for their learning activity. Some work spaces can be located within activity units, so the materials of the unit are within reach. Other work spaces can be located beside shelves or cabinets, or shelf units can be moved closer to the larger work spaces and groups of individual work spaces. In some cases, small

Booths and corners provide work spaces.

Mats can become portable work spaces.

Some children are comfortable in underneath work spaces.

Vertical and horizontal surfaces give firm support for writing or drawing.

collections of frequently used materials or tools can be stored in or on the work space, while still leaving empty space for children to work.

Learning activities that are quiet and demanding are best supported by small, sheltered work spaces, but other activities require considerable movement. The materials used for some activities are small and hand-held, while others need to be spread out. Smooth, hard surfaces may be important in some activities, and space the most important requirement for others. Spaces large enough for small groups encourage peer teaching and cooperation, but individual activities need small work spaces if they are to remain individual. The arrangement of different kinds of work spaces with some flexible enough for temporary reorganization, some permanently established, and some portable, helps support a variety of activities that can keep a group of children involved in their learning.

Display

Display facilities, the empty spaces and labels available for posting or exhibiting in the environment, make it possible for children to arrange their own displays. They are used for short periods of time, then emptied so others can use them. It takes a variety of display facilities to accommodate the different shapes, sizes, and bulk of the materials and objects children may wish to share, and several forms are especially useful: labels, stands, racks, frames, cases, bulletin boards, and shelf space. Within these groups, specific display facilities can include a variety of arrangements and objects like box lids, hanging fabric, pin-up letters, record holders, music stands, benches, and clear plastic boxes.

Different Kinds of Display Facilities

Blank strips of paper and pin-up letters serve as *labels* to support the identification of children's displayed work. Empty *stands* and *racks* of

Blank labels support identificaton of displayed work.

various sizes are useful for displaying two and three-dimensional objects. Materials for display can be set upon stands, and racks often make
it possible for children to hang their work or lay it flat.

Simple *frames* can be made with shallow boxes, paper backing, or
yarn outlines to receive children's work. *Cases* have more depth and can
display three-dimensional objects. *Bulletin boards* can be improvised by
using hanging fabric, folding screens, strips of soft wood, or cabinet
sides. Sometimes *shelf space* is available for display of bulky objects or
sets, but window ledges, benches, and partitioned boxes also offer
shelflike display space.

Stands and racks display two and three-dimensional objects.

Simple frames and cases highlight special work.

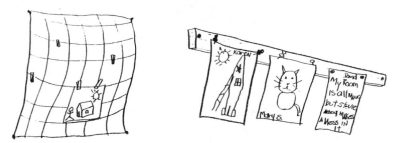

Bulletin boards can be improvised.

Window ledges and benches offer good shelf space.

Contributions of Display Facilities

Ordinarily, when children display their work so it can be seen, read, or examined by others, they don't intend to make it available for general use. A consistent use of specific locations for display helps clarify for everybody that those spaces are reserved for that purpose, and also helps children distinguish between displayed materials and materials available for free use. Label blanks, used to identify and sometimes to explain displayed materials, are equally helpful.

Display facilities for student use must be within their reach. Some built-in facilities may be only partially within reach, but these can be shared by teachers and children. On bulletin boards, borders can separate teacher display space at the top from children's space at the lower levels. Very low displays, beneath chalkboards or on the backs of low dividers, can be seen by children sitting in activity units, on the floor, or on chairs. Taller cabinet backs and sides, and standing screens, provide good display areas beside paths for children who are standing or walking. Display of three-dimensional objects requires a bit more space. Protected corners or boxlike cases work well near spaces with much movement, but somewhat less protected stands or cases serve well in quieter areas.

Provisions in a Dual Role

The teachers who developed the basic framework of the six provisioning categories were thinking about the role of the environment's provisions in children's activities for learning. They found that each of the categories supports learning activity in a particular way. *Raw materials* provide something to manipulate, shape, arrange, or combine. *Tools* make it possible for students to act upon materials or information. *Information sources* offer data in print and nonprint forms about the planned curriculum and children's interest. *Containers* arrange or store information, materials, and work in progress. *Work spaces* provide the setting where children work alone or with others, while *display facilities* encourage children to share their interests and the products of their learning activities.

In addition to supporting students' activity and enabling them to find something to do, the provisioning categories also influence learning outcomes in interesting ways. Depending on their characteristics and their function in activities, some of them influence learning by shaping content, some by eliciting skills, others by shaping the activity or stimulating continuation and depth of study.

Raw materials influence the products of children's activity. Because they tend to stimulate ideas and suggest activities, the raw materials in the environment make it possible for children to develop and extend their ideas and experience independently.

Tools suggest possibilities for action such as investigating, reorganizing materials or ideas, communicating, and preserving ideas or products. Because different tools elicit different skills, the particular tools present in the environment influence the skills that children will practice and develop.

Information sources influence the ideas and knowledge that children consider during their learning experiences and provide a focus for the use of skills and thinking processes. They shape the content of children's learning, stimulate idea connections, and capture interest, helping children to initiate and stay with productive learning activities. Information sources also elicit a variety of skills as children extract information.

Containers are by definition used for holding or storage, but their contribution to learning experiences is more complex. Since containers make it possible for children to preserve projects over a period of time and return to them, they suggest continuation of projects and study, and the planning and gathering of materials for activity to come. Through these suggestions, containers can help extend the depth of children's learning and the complexity of their work.

Work spaces support children's activities by providing appropriate spaces, and influence the kinds of interactions available by fostering the use of language, silence, cooperative study, or solitary activity, depending upon the size and amount of seclusion offered. The work spaces available to children influence the kinds of materials that can be comfortably used, and the movement that is possible during learning activities.

Display facilities provide useful communication in the learning environment, and can stimulate interest in the ideas and projects that have interested others. They also provide a context and encouragement for the self-initiated use of academic skills, as children prepare and label their own displays and examine the displays of their classmates.

Checking Your Own Environment

A Checklist of Basic Provisions is a useful tool for assessing the environment's potential support for learning activities. With this checklist, you can look at learning materials to see if there is an appropriate assortment to stimulate and maintain children's involvement in learning activities. The checklist can be used after children have left the environment, or children can work on it with you. Some teachers prefer to work with just one or two categories at a time, taking several days to gather all

A teacher's checklist of basic provisions.

the information. Remember that the checklist is applied only to materials arranged for students' direct access, not those reserved for teacher-directed instructional sessions or assignments.

1. Set up a simple checklist, identifying each of the basic provisions. Leave room to make tally marks for each item counted. This will be both guide and record as you use the checklist.
2. With the checklist in hand, move through the environment, surveying materials available to children. Count the *different kinds* in each category; duplicates don't count because you are checking assortment.
3. Make a tally mark in the appropriate category for every *kind* of object that serves the purpose of that category.
   After checking is completed, total each category.
4. Review the completed record and the totals, looking for the following information:
   — Are all categories represented?
   — Are all categories directly available to children?
   — Which categories are present in the largest assortment?
   — Which categories are underrepresented in comparison to the others?

If you need to look more closely at a particular category of provisions, check the variety of provisioning by setting up a similar checklist for that category. Just list the specific groups within that category in the left-hand column and tally in the same way. Here are the groupings within each category:

Raw materials: construction materials, natural materials, found items, fabrics, cords, papers, pigments, foods, sculpture materials.

Tools: computing, measuring, recording, joining, cutting/shaping, mixing, viewing, expressing/communicating, heating/cooling.

Information sources: references, recordings, media, labels, natural specimens, living things, models, realia, charts, pictures, books.

Containers: flats, deep containers, watertight containers, racks, envelopes, chart papers, blank books.

Work spaces: booths, corners, mats, underneaths, vertical surfaces, horizontal surfaces.

Display facilities: labels, stands, racks, frames, cases, bulletin boards, shelf space.

CHAPTER 5

PROVISIONING FOR MULTIPLE POSSIBILITIES

What children can learn from any environment is determined by the provisions available for use and their potential for learning. Some of the learning possibilities of materials selected for provisioning are related to their function in the environment. Other learning possibilities are related to the specific characteristics of the materials, such as transparency or flexibility. An audio tape, for instance, has learning potential for listening skills because it functions as an information source. It has other possibilities for learning because its spools are round, the tape winds on the spools, and the tape has texture and color, as well as the capacity to hold and give out patterns of electronic impulses. The specific characteristics can be a rich source of growth in language, intellectual processes, and conceptual development, offering multiple possibilities for learning.

The roles of different provisioning categories in children's activities have been considered in Chapter Four. It is equally useful to consider the range of opportunities for learning held by the specific materials or equipment selected within each provisioning category. Teachers can provision for maximum learning when they support children's activities with learning materials whose specific characteristics offer strong and varied learning possibilities.

The Trader

When George Kani walked into the teachers' room with two large wallpaper books under his arm, the other teachers began to laugh, asking what he wanted to trade. Almost every environment in the school had something in it that had originally come from Mr. Kani's fourth grade.

The sixth grade now had a standard fourth-grade-level dictionary in exchange for one of its copies of the world almanac. The kindergarten had a wallpaper book traded for some lined chart paper, and an abacus exchanged for an extra set of metric measuring spoons. The fifth-grade teacher had traded an old printing set for a box of print-shop paper scraps, and the art teacher was glad to offer an easel with a broken leg for some of the print-shop materials. The first and third-grade teachers had contributed a beginners' dictionary and a picture dictionary in exchange for a world map and a set of blueprints with the architect's drawings of the public library. A second-grade teacher was delighted to receive a round table with adjustable legs for four extra flat-topped desks, and the other fourth-grade teacher was glad to contribute several social studies texts from different publishers in exchange for two science-text teacher's manuals for different grade levels.

At first, the principal and some of the teachers had been concerned about a teacher's giving away materials ordered for a particular classroom. But George reminded them that everything remained in the school, after all, and was being used with children. George also offered the principal an inventory of the books, references, and other information sources in his environment, and suggested a few visits to watch children using them. The principal was convinced upon watching a child who was unable to find a word in one dictionary move on to a second and a third, persisting until the word was located. Mr. Kani's inventory showed fifteen different dictionaries in the environment, including at least one traded from each grade level, a Spanish-English dictionary, the American Heritage dictionary, and several other junior and adult editions. Some children needed assistance in reading the definitions in the adult editions, but they were able to find the entries. The principal observed that for spelling information, any dictionary containing the word would do, but children seemed to prefer the definitions in the adult dictionaries, which were more specific and also more elaborate.

For a long time Mr. Kani's fourth grade looked quite different from other environments in the school. There was a remarkable variety of material available for student use each day. Then, as George continued to make exchanges with teachers, other environments began to show more variety, too. The assortment of raw materials expanded as teachers traded plasticine for styrofoam, newsprint for tracing paper, wood scraps for computer paper. Collections of tools became more varied as teachers began to exchange one linear measuring tool for another, magnifying glasses for number lines, masking tape for library paste, and chalk for grease pencils. Information sources, furniture to arrange variations in work spaces, and potential display facilities were also exchanged.

Mr. Kani's environment still seemed to have more diversified provisioning than most, and the teachers were fascinated by the interesting things he offered to share with them. A set of pulleys, a model of a human heart, wooden letters, film cans, maps, seed collections, blueprints, medicine vials, and rug samples were only some of the materials he had to share. Many came from local shops, agencies, businesses, and service companies where George checked regularly to ask what materials were available for children's use at school.

Now and then a teacher would ask if George ever became tired of his continual hunting for provisions and trading with other classrooms, but he didn't seem to mind the time or effort: there were so many possibilities for learning, he told them, that it was well worth it. Wherever the children went in the environment, they were confronted by something to do, and by something that could be learned from doing it.

The Possibilities of Variety

Children can encounter daily many learning opportunities that are present because of the variety of materials within each provisioning category. The opportunity to use, to see variations, and to find commonalities among various forms of similar materials and equipment opens possibilities for language growth, thinking and concept elaboration, skill development, and creativity.

Language

Specific labels and descriptive terms used to name and describe the environment's provisions can hold strong possibilities for vocabulary extension. When words are first encountered in the context of a material's use, meaning is reinforced, and opportunities to use the words in

Twenty-four containers of glue are labeled with the same vocabulary as one.

The labels for different kinds of adhesives hold many vocabulary possibilities.

purposeful ways are offered. If a choice of tools or materials is available, there are many possible methods for creating a project. Precise language and accurate terms are needed to explain which were used, and why.

Twenty-four containers of white latex glue can be labeled and described with exactly the same vocabulary as one container. The labels for mucilage, whipped library paste, rubber cement, or a glue stick, and the differences in color, texture, density, drying time, strength, and solubility of these adhesives, offer larger and more diverse vocabulary possibilities. Containers designed to hold liquids have different characteristics from containers for dry materials even when made of similar materials, as for instance the clay in ceramic vases and clay flower pots. Such containers offer several language-learning possibilities as children examine differences and attempt to describe or explain them. When a choice of joining techniques is offered by available materials, there are several ways to assemble a book. An accurate vocabulary is needed to explain it to others.

There is language-learning potential in the differences among related materials.

An accurate vocabulary is needed to explain how a book was constructed.

Thinking and Concepts

Possibilities for challenging thought appear when there are several different forms of materials or tools for similar purposes. Comparisons of different forms, speculations about the function or purposes of variations and predictions about the effects of particular forms can be made. Children may see relationships between different kinds of material used in the learning environment, and other variations encountered elsewhere. Developing concepts of function and attributes also requires variety, so that children can see and experience the common characteristics of a group of tools such as cutting tools, or encounter many examples of a single attribute like smoothness among many different kinds of provisions. The elaboration of more complex concepts, as for instance that people have developed ways to preserve and share information across time, is made possible through a variety of materials. Through multiple experiences with these materials, children can encounter the idea in a number of different contexts.

The varied forms of shaping tools offer possibilities for thinking processes. It seems natural to compare the roughness of sandpaper with the sharpness of a carpenter's plane and the evenness of a putty knife, as each tool is used to produce a smooth surface. The smooth point on an awl, the spiraling grooves of a drill bit, and the blunt end of a hole punch are different, inviting children to think about functional reasons for each.

Many information sources are examples of the way people store and share ideas with one another. Records, historical certificates, charts,

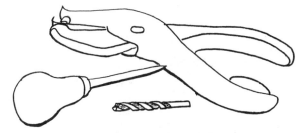

**Children can think about functional reasons for differences
among cutting tools.**

maps, drawings, and architectural models all promote a richer and deeper understanding of that concept than books alone can offer.

Understanding of linear measurement grows through using a variety of tools. Measuring the circumference of a ball is difficult with a straight-edged rule; more flexible tools make it easier. Short, calibrated measures useful for drawings and models aren't accurate for larger dimensions like the length of a classroom, but a carpenter's steel tape rule does very well. Each tool offers a different context for an experience with linear measurement, and with each new context the concepts grow more elaborate.

Skills

The amount of child-initiated practice that occurs for a variety of skills, from sequencing to writing, listening, and observing, depends on the environment's provisions. Tools, which make action possible, elicit the physical and academic skills related to their functions. Information sources call upon the skills to retrieve the information they hold. Raw

**Varied information sources help children understand complex
concepts of information storage.**

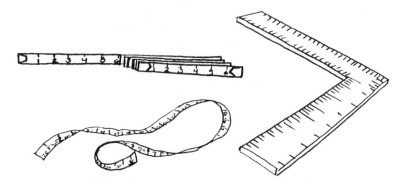

**Understanding measurement requires experiences with varied tools
in different contexts.**

materials generate the use of skills as they are explored, changed, and manipulated, and display facilities offer motivation to use skills for labeling, explaining processes, or sharing information. The greater the variety of provisions, the greater the possibilites for skill development.

A good, comprehensive book about frogs may hold enough information to answer most questions about frogs, but it does limit learning potential if it is the only resource on the topic. Opportunities to extract and test information about frogs from a picture file, an encyclopedia, microscope slides, a diagram, trade books, a filmstrip, and the living organisms themselves invite the use of many different skills. Observations of physical change can be recorded in writing or by a sequence of drawings, by tallies on a record sheet, or by a photograph, tape recording, graph, or diagram. Each process requires skills, and

**Extracting information from different information sources
uses many skills.**

Varied materials let children record events within their own skill levels.

variety in materials offers children opportunity to record within the abilities of their own skill development level. Construction materials have possibilities for measurement, computation, and recording skills, when the accompanying materials suggest drawing plans, researching information, or interpreting someone else's directions and plans. Models, play constructions, stage scenery, and working constructions like shelves or wagons all need different kinds of planning and levels of accuracy.

The skills of locating information through alphabetical order can be used daily, if variety in provisioning offers the need. Files for students'

Construction materials have potential for computation and
recording skills.

Variety can establish the need for alphabetizing skills.

daily work folders, city or town maps, almanacs, class lists for student reference, community directories, telephone books, mail order catalogues, picture and article files all call for the use of alphabetical order.

Creativity

When choices of materials and process are available through provisioning, many possibilities to express creativity are available. Variety in the texture, sizes, colors, and other characteristics of raw materials offers individual variation in children's projects. There are many ways to gather information, arrange a collection, bind a book, or report and share information. Variety in tools, materials, and information sources allows individual children to express their inventiveness. As children develop skills with conventions of writing, computation, inquiry, and language, options for the use of tools and materials can offer possibilities for creativity within the same learning activities that call for the use of these conventions.

When recording or reporting in sequence, a person orders events as they occurred in time, but the reporting can be done in different ways. Calendar notations, a series of drawings, talking into a tape recorder, graphing, writing, and drawing with overlays are possible creative approaches when varied tools and materials are there to suggest and support them.

Stories are written to be read, which requires accepted letter forms, spellings, and other conventions of print. But a story can be bound in book form in several ways, mounted and displayed in the author's own way, typed, written on lined paper, or lettered with marking pens. Illustrations may accompany a story, and the design and placement of the illustrations and print offer creative possibilities.

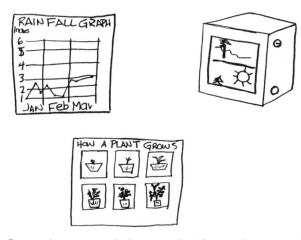

Sequencing means ordering events but they can be reported in different ways.

Writing stories requires conventions of print, but there are many ways to illustrate them.

Selecting Materials for Holding Power

The learning possibilities of the environment's provisions are realized only when children become involved with the materials, staying with them long enough to encounter their possibilities. If materials with holding power are included in the environment's provisioning, the likelihood is strong that children will work in some depth and move toward a variety of learnings.

Materials with fairly high complexity keep children involved, lengthen their attention span, and reduce the need for adult direction and

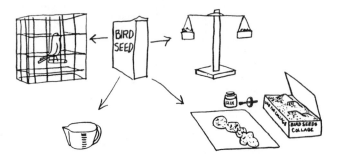

Bulk materials used in many settings add complexity.

help with learning activities.[1] The amount of complexity offered by materials or by an activity unit depends on the number of different options for actions presented by the materials. Complex materials hold many options for activity, while simple materials offer a single activity possibility.[2] When an environment has a predominance of simple materials, it's difficult for the materials to hold children's attention for any length of time because there are few choices for action.

Most of the complexity in the environment comes from combinations of materials within activity units, as described in Chapter Seven. However, sometimes there are differences in the complexity of the materials themselves. Some materials are simple, having just one obvious use, but others are complex because they have subparts to be used in different ways, or they encourage improvising, or they have a certain amount of unpredictability.[3]

Multiuse materials can contribute to complexity of many areas and activity units. They lend themselves to use in several different settings and combinations because they can be acted upon by different tools and processes. The selection of complex and multiuse materials can build holding power into the environment through complexity.

Bulk raw materials like pebbles, sand and dried beans can be used in many different settings and play many different roles in learning activities. Such materials add complexity to many activity units in combination with dramatic props, tools for observation and testing, art materials, and some kinds of measurement tools.

[1]*Sybil Kritchevsky, Elizabeth Prescott, and Lee Walling,* Planning Environments for Young Children: Physical Space, *2nd ed. (Washington, D.C.: National Association for the Education of Young Children, 1977), pp. 11–17.*

[2]*Elizabeth Jones,* Dimensions of Teaching-Learning Environments: Handbook for Teachers *(Pasadena: Pacific Oaks College Bookstore, 1973), pp. 11–12.*

[3]*Kritchevsky, Prescott, and Walling,* Planning Environments, p. 11.

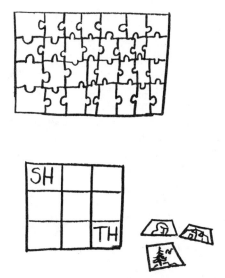

Single-use materials don't keep children involved very long.

Single-use materials such as matching games and jigsaw puzzles are simple materials; they are useful and enjoyable, but don't keep children involved very long or very often. On the other hand, a set of blocks offers many options for activity because there are so many subparts that can be combined in different ways. Their complexity holds children's interest for long periods of time.

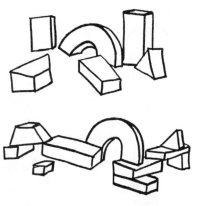

A set of blocks offers many options; their complexity holds children's interest.

Reflecting the Community

Many children leave one world and enter another every day as they move from home to school. The contrast is greatest when there are marked cultural differences between learning in the community and in school environments, but those differences exist to some degree in all communities. They affect the learning possibilities of the environment through their influence on children's feelings of comfort and their attitudes as they approach learning materials.

Teachers can build reflections of the community into the learning environment through provisioning. As the teacher uses the community as a source of noncatalogue materials, the environment begins to resemble the community a little. Materials from community businesses or industry, loaned or contributed materials from children's homes, and locally purchased objects that might be found in households can all offer affective strength to the environment's learning possibilities.

Community reflections are also built by exercising judgment in provisioning, so that any strong community or cultural attitudes are respected, and children can be comfortable in the environment. Many teachers can give examples of strong community attitudes that affect children's feelings about learning materials.

One science teacher new to a Southwestern community that did not explain its ways to outsiders, learned about the community's attitudes toward remains of once-living animals through a provisioning decision. The teacher brought two animal skeletons into the environment, with some activity cards for bones from a commercial science kit. As soon as the students came in and saw the materials, it was clear that something was wrong. Instead of exploring the materials with interest, as the teacher expected, the students grew very quiet and moved away. A mixture of tension, embarrassment, and avoidance showed how uncomfortable they were. When the teacher removed the skeletons from the environment, things returned to normal and everyone was able to settle down to work. In the culture of that community, caged animals and natural specimens of once-living creatures are regarded as unapproachable.

Water and some foods like rice or flour are often useful raw materials for experimentation or creative activities, but in certain communities their use in the environment is inappropriate. In areas suffering water shortage, conservation may be so essential that community attitudes toward casual use of water don't permit its use in the classroom. Some small rural communities where the people labored hard for many years to raise food in difficult soil, traditionally view the use of food in exploration activities as a waste. Provisioning can reflect the community

Familiar wildflowers attract children's interest.

when the teacher comes to know the community makes judgments based on that knowledge. The selection of information sources, raw materials, and other provisions requires such judgment wherever strong attitudes and traditions exist.

Provisioning that reflects the community can help children see that what is offered in school is also useful in their out-of-school lives. By reflecting children's personal lives, the environment offers a message of acceptance and welcome to the children who come to work in it. This makes it possible for individuals to connect their learning out in the community with the learning that occurs in the school setting, so each can build upon the other.

Local plants and wild flowers offer familiarity and attract children's interest. At the same time they may offer information previously unnoticed, as they stay available for observation through the processes of

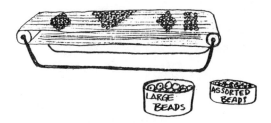

Materials reflecting community crafts create bonds between home and school.

Natural materials from the community are useful counters.

budding, blooming, fading, petal dropping, and seed production. Raw materials that reflect the arts or working crafts of the community are also useful learning materials, creating a bond between the daily lives of children outside school, and the work and setting of the learning environment.

Some learning materials like counting objects don't necessarily require any particular form. Instead of catalogue-ordered counting objects, children could be using seashells, stones, seed pods, or other objects from their own community environment. In addition, information sources such as photographs and natural materials contributed from home surroundings can engage the children's natural interests and motivations.

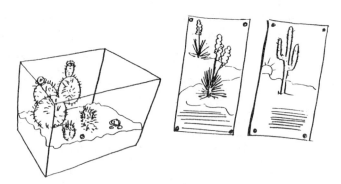

Information sources from home surroundings engage interest.

Finding Learning Materials

A big part of most schools' budgets for instructional materials is used to purchase textbooks and supplementary materials for planned direct instruction in the environment, which limits the funds left for other materials. Yet the environment still needs to be provisioned with supplies and equipment for children's use during the independent learning experiences that occur during a school day. There are ways to find low-cost and no-cost learning materials to supplement the school-purchased supplies and expand the learning possibilities for children.

Trading

Trading makes a good beginning for expanded provisioning. When teachers within a school trade materials, the environments of all participants tend to change, since trading involves exchange of desired materials by people who want something to improve their own settings. The trading teacher described at the beginning of this chapter had gradually built variety into his learning environment and helped others do the same. Planning ahead for trading sometimes makes coordinated ordering of materials possible, as teachers plan to purchase and subdivide bulk orders of various consumable materials. Exchanges of furniture and equipment from time to time can also help expand learning possibilities within individual environments.

In some schools teachers plan to share the work of gathering free and inexpensive materials that can then move into several environments through trading. Teachers' Centers often assist in the gathering and sharing of donated materials for groups of teachers across several different schools or districts. Teachers can contribute their surplus supply of one kind of material in exchange for another.

Loaned Materials

The best-known sources of loaned materials are libraries. In addition to books, many school, town, or state libraries circulate audio recordings, art reproductions, and picture files for classrooms. In some large cities teachers can check out collections of museum materials such as artifacts, natural specimens, documents, charts, models, and realia. On state and regional levels there are often associations such as state dairy councils, historical societies, and dental associations that lend sets of materials. Large school systems may gather publishers' demonstration materials in curriculum centers where teachers can check them out. Teachers' Centers are also good loan sources for commercial, teacher-made, and special collections of learning materials.

Libraries often lend nonprint information sources.

Some loaned materials come from professionals working in private practice or within larger organizations who can lend information sources like anatomical models, or engineering drawings related to the local area. The school itself is a good source for loaned materials from the cafeteria, the nurse's office, or the custodian's room. Families sometimes lend pictures, souvenirs, collections, and tools. All these materials add learning possibilities to the environment.

Bargain Shopping

A quick walk through a variety store, household department, or hardware store reveals many materials and small tools useful for children's learning. But a small amount of money can go much further at a flea market, garage sale, thrift shop, or rummage sale where many of the same things, some new and some used, are sold for just a few cents apiece. Large communities often have surplus stores and odd-lot stores that offer new merchandise at exceptionally low prices.

Some military installations, public institutions (including large school systems and hospitals), and government agencies offer old materials and obsolete parts or broken equipment for sale in their warehouses or salvage yards. Usually these places give priority to groups and individuals within their organizations, but periodically they are open to the public. Salvage and surplus yards offer very interesting raw materials and other provisions, varying with the work of the organization.

Flea markets and garage sales sell materials for learning.

Teachers' Centers sometimes offer very inexpensive classroom materials purchased for minimum cost from local businesses or industries.

Donated Materials

In most communities there are businesses, shops, agencies, and institutions that have much material to offer the learning environment. Some of these produce information sources like brochures, posters, booklets, maps, and charts. Other potential sources discard materials each day that could be very helpful for children's learning, from building plans to empty film spools, computer paper, or obsolete highway signs. Utility companies, retail shops, personal service shops, repair businesses, medical offices, manufacturing plants, shipping and transportation companies, federal agencies, information-processing companies, and city or county offices are some of the community resources that can donate materials for the learning environment.

Often, people discard materials without being aware of their possibilities for children's learning. If teachers help them become aware of the usefulness of materials, many business people are happy to donate them for children's use. Sometimes teachers find resources and materials they hadn't anticipated, as helpful business people suggest additional materials or places to search.

Some teachers are not comfortable with the idea of scrounging around the community, asking for free materials, until the first successful interaction. Going with another teacher is a helpful way to get started, and the interest and cooperativeness of most local people soon makes a teacher more comfortable. Such forays into the community also give

Community businesses have material for provisioning.

opportunity for teachers to talk informally with community members about the good things happening in their children's learning. Materials acquired in this way have special possibilities for provisioning: they reflect the children's community and so play a role in children's learning that most catalogue materials cannot.

Checking Your Community's Resources

It is possible to check your community's resources for learning by using the Yellow Pages of the telephone book to find institutions, retail outlets, professional offices, public agencies, and other businesses that may have materials to contribute. If you live in a rural area, you may want to use the phone book from the trading community where most of the school's families do major shopping. If you live in a large urban area, you can focus on the business community nearest the school.

1. First, spend some time looking through the Yellow Pages, familiarizing yourself with the main headings. Think about the kinds of organizations connected with each heading, about their purposes and the materials associated with them. Make note of the headings that look most promising.
2. Set up a record sheet that will help you note specific information about the organizations under each heading.
3. Go back to the promising headings one at a time and begin to identify particular businesses within the community that may have materials

BUSINESS	POSSIBLE MATERIAL	LOAN/GIFT	POSSIBLE PROVISION CATEGORY	OTHER INFORMATION
BERNALILLO FEED STORE	BROCHURES ABOUT STOCK ANIMALS FEED SAMPLES PICTURES/CHARTS ON ANIMAL NUTRITION PACKING MATERIAL CHICKS- FERTILE EGGS	GIVEN SOME LENT (LENT)	INFORMATION SOURCES RAW MATERIALS CONTAINERS	CAN ON FRIDAYS - TO SEE WHATS AVAILABLE
CUSTOM SHUTTER COMPANY	WOOD SCRAPS DESIGN DRAWINGS HARDWARE SAMPLES BROCHURES PRICE LISTS STAIN SAMPLES WOOD SAMPLES	GIVEN	INFORMATION SOURCES RAW MATERIALS	
JIFFY FREIGHT COMPANY	PACKING			

Checking possibilities in the Yellow Pages.

to offer. Make note of the specific entries. Note also whether you think they may have scrap pieces, emptied containers, surplus or obsolete materials, information to disseminate, samples, models, or advertising samples.

4. Review the entries you have listed on the record sheet and also note the following:
   — Which provisioning categories might each one offer (raw materials, tools, information sources, containers, work spaces, display facilities)?
   — Is the material most likely to be given or lent to teachers?

Once your own list is completed, check out your thinking by contacting the places directly. Usually a personal visit is more productive than a phone call. Don't be discouraged if you don't find materials the first time you ask; try another source. Then try the first place again after a week or two, if you think the people might be willing, but were simply unfamiliar with the school use possibilities of their material.

SECTION III

ARRANGING LEARNING MATERIALS

CHAPTER 6

ARRANGEMENT AND DISPLAY

Arranging learning materials is sometimes seen as a housekeeping task, just a matter of establishing order, but it's much more than that—a way of getting materials into the hands of learners, where they can support activities and promote learning. Materials can't affect learning unless they are used, and if children don't see or can't reach them, materials won't be used much without teacher direction.

Children scan the environment as they move through it and look around periodically while engaged in activities. Their scanning brings them a good deal of information about the environment's provisions and about possibilities for their use. What children see as they scan affects their ideas and activities in powerful ways. If the learning materials are carefully organized and displayed so the materials and their attributes are clearly visible, they can suggest activities. Well-displayed materials can also suggest connections, offer information and remind children that they can extend their learning activities.

Visually clear arrangements put materials to work so children will receive continuous invitations to learning. Within the same arrangements, materials can be placed so children can reach or handle them or take them elsewhere. This helps children identify, locate, reach, assemble, carry, use, and replace materials without teacher assistance. Arrangements for visual clarity and physical access make it possible for children to return and replace materials as easily as they can get them, so materials remain in order and available for use.

Sometimes children seem disinterested in some materials, or careless and even destructive in using and replacing others. It's easy to mistake the effects of display for children's true habits or preferences, but more often than not, apparent carelessness or disinterest is related to materials arrangement. Clear display arrangements call attention to significant qualities of learning materials, and facilitate children's ability to reach and use them. Without clear display it is difficult for children to find and care for materials appropriately. It may even be difficult for children to notice some materials, although they would find them extremely attractive if they could be seen.

The Games Shelf

By the end of the first month of school, Gayle Malloy and Irene Begay, teachers who shared a learning environment with fifty-three primary children, were really exasperated. The classroom area where they had arranged games, puzzles, and other manipulatives was left in disorder each day. Children were reliable about cleaning up in other areas of the environment, but the shelves were a jumble of lost pieces, mixed-up sets, torn boxes, and small parts spilled out onto the shelves and nearby floor.

The game area was in a ten-foot-long shelf unit containing three twelve-inch-deep shelves. Each set of material was in its own box, with a large manuscript label written on the side. Commercial materials were stored in the decorated boxes in which they had been received, and teacher-made sets were kept in shoe, hosiery, or stationery boxes.

At first, the teachers stacked the closed boxes on the shelves, thinking that clearly written labels would help children identify each set. Before long, the ends of the boxes were bent or crushed. The teachers understood how that happened when they saw children at the shelves bending up lid corners to peek inside. Other children moved the covered boxes back and forth to tables, carrying them, uncovering them, looking

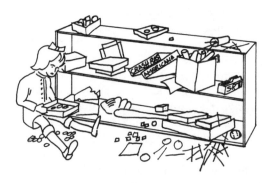

The shelves were a jumble.

inside, returning one box and selecting another, until they found the specific set they needed. Obviously, the labels hadn't provided much information. Nor did children understand how parts of sets were used together, even though simple directions were written inside the box lids; they often asked for help.

The teachers had rearranged the materials once. They unstacked them and placed them side by side, uncovered, so the contents of each box and its outside label could be seen. After that, children seemed to locate materials more easily, but they also spilled more on the shelves, and on the way to the tables where they used the materials. Lost pieces had to be hunted down, and the last-minute pickup rush resulted in small parts being tossed hurriedly into open boxes, so that pieces often ended up with the wrong set.

It was clear that some changes were needed, either in rules for use of the materials or in the arrangement of the area where they were stored. The teachers agreed that removing the manipulatives was not an option: each set was in the environment because it had learning potential, but obviously it had to be complete. The teachers briefly considered controlling the handling of the materials by giving them to children for use at specific times of the day, but decided against this because there just wasn't enough teacher time. So their problem solving concentrated on the arrangement of materials.

One afternoon after school the teachers sat on the floor to look over the games shelf, trying to see the materials as the children saw them. To their surprise, they found that different sets of materials looked alike. Each box held several pieces of cardboard or small, brightly colored pieces of plastic or wood. No single part of any set had enough information on it to show its function, or to indicate the set it belonged to.

When the teachers tried to replace some spilled pieces, it was impossible to tell what some of them were. A two-inch tagboard square with a numeral on it could have belonged to any one of several teacher-made sets. Gayle found some loose pieces from an Animal Lotto game, but it took several minutes to locate the right box on the shelf to put the pieces away.

Quickly scanning the shelf, Irene discovered that she needed to read labels to know what was in a box, even when the boxes were open to show the materials. Yet both teachers were aware that their six, seven, and eight-year-olds weren't yet automatic readers, and depended on seeing materials more than reading labels to find out what was available. Then, while shifting boxes from one shelf to another, the teachers spilled several pieces. Each box had been filled so full that small parts fell out over the sides.

It wasn't easy to see which box held which materials.

Basically, the problem of lost and ruined materials seemed to result from the way materials were boxed and how they were displayed on the shelves. The teachers needed a new arrangement to make materials visible, easier to use, and simple to carry. The new arrangement, however, required more than rearranging the existing boxes on the shelves. The learning materials needed new holders, each one distinct from the others, so children could easily identify the right materials among many that looked alike. The new holders must show their contents clearly and organize sets of materials to indicate how different parts could be used together. At the same time, each holder needed to function as a carrier designed to eliminate the spilling of small parts.

Holders and Organizers

Teachers control the appearance of materials in the learning environment through their selection of the holders in which the materials will be organized and displayed. Some teachers make conscious decisions about this, transferring materials into special containers they have made or acquired. But other teachers leave the materials packaged as received.

Packaging used for selling, storing, and shipping educational materials is usually bright, compact, and tightly closed. When materials are

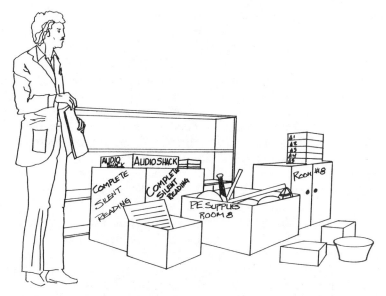

Teachers can control the appearance of materials with organizers.

packed in sets or in bulk, many pieces are put into as small a container as possible, with no wasted space. Each box is filled completely, then covered and perhaps sealed, to keep the materials confined. Often containers are meant to be stacked in storage or shipping, so flat surfaces are used to make them stackable. Covers are bright and attractive, with pictures or labels to describe the contents. Some companies use the same design on all their boxes, and only the printed labels on lid and sides give information about contents.

Materials need a different kind of holder when they are displayed for teaching purposes. Classroom holders and organizers can sort and separate objects, group diverse materials, show attributes, and make it easier to reach and carry the materials. The holders and organizers need to be as varied as the kinds of materials children use for learning.

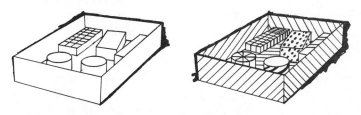

Plain holders highlight materials, but decorations camouflage them.

Manufactured containers like divided trays, storage bins, or baskets are useful for some materials. Trays, boxes, bins, and carriers can be created from shipping cartons, and racks can be built or adapted from other equipment.

A good holder highlights the material it displays, rather than focusing attention on itself. To do this, holders must be undecorated, with plain rather than patterned surfaces. Patterned holders tend to camouflage the materials they contain, because they bombard the viewer's eye with more information than the materials themselves.

Some textures and colors are better than others for highlighting materials. Natural materials like wood and straw offer a calm and attractive background to set off materials. Trays and boxes painted in deep, clear colors highlight the bright colors of materials like cuisinaire rods or parquetry blocks. Grayed or softened tones absorb the colors and make the same materials less noticeable. The smooth, clear, deep colors of some plastic storage bins and trays designed for homes or industry can be very effective organizers. The best colors and textures for a holder are determined by the materials to be displayed and the qualities to be highlighted.

Effective holders and organizers are usually roomy in relation to the materials displayed. When each holder provides enough room to spread out a group of materials or to separate different kinds of objects, the attributes of three-dimensional materials can be shown clearly. Children can carry materials if the holders are high enough to keep objects from falling out over the sides, and roomy enough to hold all the material without a special packing design.

Most holders and organizers are open, so the materials they contain can be seen. They are shelved without covers, and their contents can be seen with a glance down into the holder. Some have one open end or side, so materials are visible when the tops of the holders are hidden. Others are transparent, showing their contents even when placed above eye level. The form of openness needed in any particular organizer depends on the materials to be contained, and on the height of their location on the shelves of a storage unit.

Holders that provide a focusing background for learning materials highlight the materials well. Such holders are practical and functional, and also aesthetically pleasing. The appearance and the interesting attributes of the materials will create a beautiful setting that invites and encourages learning.

It takes many different holders to display the materials of any learning environment. Open, boxlike holders are useful for a variety of materials and sets. Bins with open ends, to hold bulk materials, can be made from cartons, or purchased. Bowls and baskets show several sides

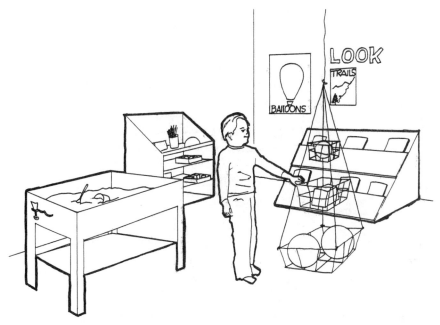

Most holders and organizers are open.

of objects placed inside them, and trays or other low organizers exhibit an array of objects very well. Racks attached to a vertical surface or placed on a shelf display the faces of materials, and a few tall holders can display long items like paint brushes or rolls of paper.

Providing Visual Access to Materials

Unless children can see materials as they scan the environment, they aren't likely to think about using them. Taking the materials out of the closet is one way to make them more visible. Another way is to open boxes and reorganize the materials so that no parts are hidden. The visibility created by those simple steps is part of any arrangement designed to make children aware of learning materials and their uses. Effective display also requires visual clarity, provided by arrangements that focus attention on the most significant characteristics of each learning material, so that materials can be perceived and identified at a glance.

Children and adults tend to perceive the learning environment differently because they see it from different heights and places. It is what the children see, rather than what the teacher sees, that determines visual clarity. Checking materials arrangement for its visual clarity

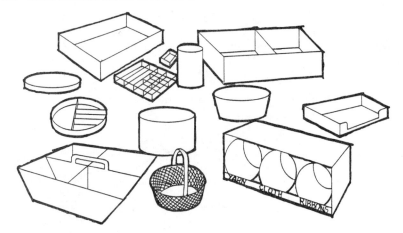

Many different holders and organizers display materials.

means scanning the material from the child's eye level and work places. Children's eye levels, the places from which they will view materials, and the customary paths by which they move through the environment affect what they can and can't see. A material holder that offers a view of its contents at one shelf height or location can conceal them at another. For instance, materials in open boxes above children's eye level can't be seen, while on a lower shelf they can be. Shelving behind a screen doesn't provide much visibility, but materials placed on shelves beside paths can be seen by everybody who passes by.

The important qualities of one type of learning material can be very different from those of another. Different materials require somewhat different arrangements for visibility. Some materials like patterned paper or books carry information across their faces, and need arrangements that make the entire face visible. On the other hand, materials like construction paper, modeling clay, and counting blocks show their important attributes when only a portion of the material is visible.

A visually clear arrangement for learning materials offers a calm, unpatterned background and surrounds each set of displayed material with empty space. Because the visual stimuli from the background are held to a minimum, the important qualities of the material can be seen at a glance. Busy patterned covering on shelf surfaces or holders can create visual confusion and make it difficult to focus on the materials. In almost the same way, tightly packed shelves with stacked containers and no spacing between materials also limit the visibility of specific items.

Achieving visual clarity in the arrangement of materials requires restraint. In many environments shelf space for learning materials seems to be at a premium, yet the effect of generous spacing and separation on the number of materials actually used for learning is powerful. Almost always, fewer materials placed on the shelves means that more materials from those shelves will be used, because they can be seen and identified. Material display can be expanded with racks and hangers for face-out display, with additional shelves in some storage units, and by rotation of materials from closets to display shelves.

Making Materials Visible

Uncovering boxes of material is a good beginning for visibility. Open boxes show the top layer of materials inside, but if there is more than one layer, some of the materials in the box are still invisible. Similarly, stacked materials are hidden materials except for the item on top, but some of the materials become visible when the layers are separated by space between layers.

There is more than one way to stack materials. Side-by-side stacking hides the information across the face of materials. Some commonly stacked materials show very little information from the sides or edges; books, records, and puzzles all offer information across the front. Obviously, then, it helps to change the position of books and materials so that illustrations, print, and other information on the face can be seen.

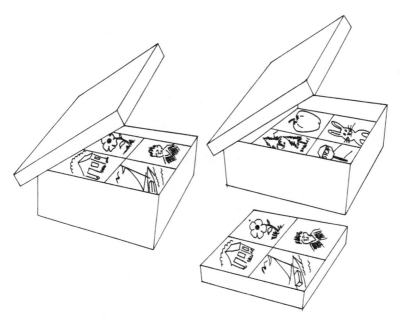

Uncovering boxes shows only the top layer of material.

Stacked materials are hidden, but separating the layers shows them.

Side-by-side stacking hides the information across the front.

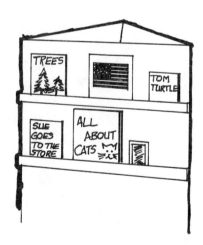

Book and records can be arranged to show their faces.

Shelf height affects the visibility of materials.

Shelf height affects the visibility of materials; above children's eye level, uncovering isn't enough: children still see only the sides of boxes. Transparent holders and organizers allow materials at eye level or above to be seen. Shelves at waist level display materials inside open holders, even when these are deep. Materials on the lowest shelves are most visible in low, traylike holders that display materials toward the front edges of the shelf, where they aren't hidden by the shelves above.

Focus on Materials

When a collection of various objects is spread across a shelf, the materials are all visible, but it's hard to tell just what particular items are there, because there are so many. Sorting and grouping the materials gives more information about the contents of the shelf. Moving groups away from one another sets off each grouping and makes it more noticeable. The larger the empty space around it, the more clearly attention is focused on a grouping.

Even clearer focus on materials results when a group of objects is placed within an enclosing form like a tray or low box. An enclosing

Transparent holders and organizers show materials at eye level.

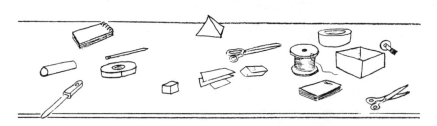

When objects are spread across a shelf, specific items don't show clearly.

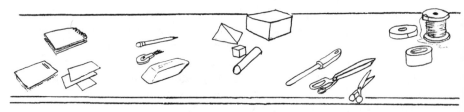

Grouping and separating materials makes them more noticeable.

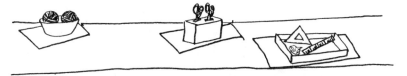

Empty space around groups of materials focuses attention.

A tray or a circle of yarn keeps objects in an enclosing form.

form can also be created by surrounding material with a circle of contrasting yarn or cord, and by fastening colored tape or shapes of contrasting paper to the shelf surface.

Differentiating Similar Materials

Commercial boxes containing sets of materials look very much alike. But the sets themselves, once removed from the boxes and arranged in holders that are quite distinct, appear much less alike.

Children can identify specific sets of materials easily when they are displayed in holders large enough to show all the parts clearly. Moving

Sets in commercial boxes look alike.

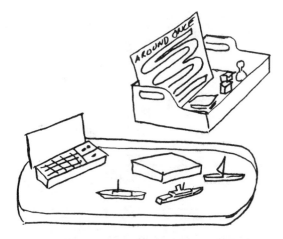

**Materials removed from commercial boxes look different
in different holders.**

Holders that display all parts of a set make identification easy.

Separating similar materials is helpful.

similar materials away from one another is also helpful, since varied surroundings help differentiate materials. Several different locations around the environment can display similar materials and still provide access.

Providing Physical Access to Materials

Most arrangements for visual clarity of materials can also improve physical access, if both needs are considered at the time the materials are arranged. Ample spacing between shelved items makes it easy to remove one set of materials without knocking over another, and also facilitates return of the materials after use. Unstacking materials to display them also permits children to reach one piece of material without having to shift others first. Materials placed with consideration for children's eye level are also well within the children's reach.

There are also other ways to arrange for children's physical access to materials. Each holder for learning materials can also serve as a carrier. The shape, size, and weight of the materials will determine the style and proportions of the carrier. Handles cut into large carriers make it possible for children to carry without tipping or spilling the materials.

Decentralizing the materials display by separating and relocating similar materials in different areas tends to reduce traffic congestion at shelf units. Children can pick up and return materials without crowding, jostling, or bumping elbows. Decentralization is especially useful for physical access to materials like playground equipment that are needed by many people at the same time of day.

Arranging for Reach Level

Collections placed in trays on shelves at children's shoulder level or higher tend to tip and spill when removed, whereas materials arranged on low trays are easy for children to lift. When hooks for hanging articles are above the children's reach they can still remove the articles fairly easily as long as they can grasp the bottom of the hanging objects. But children must be able to touch the hooks with their fingers to hang the materials up. When materials are stacked, children need to lift and shift the top layers to get at those below; two hands aren't enough to do this easily.

Arranging for Easy Carrying

When materials, accessories, and cleanup equipment are combined in a single carrier, children can locate everything they need without extra searching or traveling. Holders for display can be designed so children

Trays on high shelves spill easily.

Materials on trays are easy to lift from low shelves.

To hang objects, the hooks need to be within finger reach.

Stacked materials require shifting and lifting.

can carry materials easily and safely. But holders that are easy for adult fingers to grasp may be awkward for the smaller hands of children.

Tall or standing articles like pitchers are apt to tip or spill when carried in shallow holders. Placing tall items in holders that are deep enough to minimize falling out makes carrying much simpler, though the materials should still be visible. Puzzles and other materials to be assembled can be placed in a holder large enough for assembly; parts

Cleanup equipment combined in a single carrier is easier to locate and use.

Holders for display can be used to carry materials.

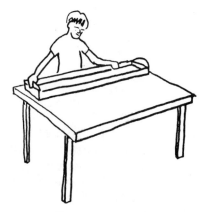

Holders easy for adults may be awkward for children to grasp.

Tall articles can tip or spill in shallow holders.

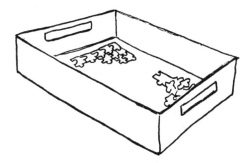

Handles cut into the sides help children carry larger holders.

won't be dropped or lost, and work in progress can be preserved until later. Handles cut into the sides of the larger holders help children carry them level and minimize spilling. Since it's difficult not to spill pieces when boxes are filled to the brim, making sure that holders are larger than the materials to be carried will cut down on accidents and loss of parts.

Facilitating Return of Materials

It's easy to find the place where a holder and its material belong, when shelf locations are marked with tape. Consistent placement of each organizer is helped by labeling and by spaces between the holders, so that everybody can check the shelves quickly at the end of the day to see that everything is in place.

Clustering materials in a single area of the environment often causes congestion, jostling, and spilling at the shelves; this can be prevented by locating commonly used materials in several different areas. Also, it seems easier to remember where particular materials belong, when holders and organizers are distinctive and clearly display the materials; special materials belong in special locations.

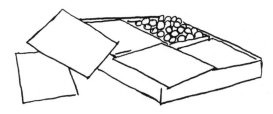

Parts spill easily from boxes filled to the brim.

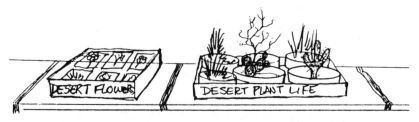

Shelves marked with tape show where materials belong.

Clustering many materials in one place can cause congestion.

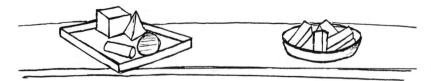

It's easier to remember where materials belong when they don't all look alike.

Display to Clarify Activity

Sets designed for a particular activity usually have two or three different forms of material, each with a specific use in the activity. Generally the parts are kept together, but it isn't always clear without teacher assistance how the parts are used or what activity is intended. Sets can be displayed so that the appearance of the materials gives children some idea of intended use and of relationships between parts. Small containers can hold some parts within a larger organizer containing the complete set. When sets include several different forms of material, the small containers may be selected—like the larger holder— to highlight important qualities of the parts they display.

Sometimes teachers design projects, experiments, and activities requiring more than one kind of material. The needed combination of raw materials, tools, and protective and cleanup equipment assembled in an organizer can support children's satisfaction and success in carrying out the activity. Focusing attention on the component parts of the set of materials conveys information about relationships between them and about possible uses.

Different sets of materials to be used together are sometimes packaged separately. Stringing beads, wooden cubes or parquetry blocks often have accompanying sets of design cards that are boxed separately. Using these materials involves reproducing two-dimensional patterns with three-dimensional objects. Because of their separate boxes, the connection between the materials isn't very clear. When wooden cubes are displayed in their own holder, in the same large box that shows matching pattern cards, activity possibilities are clarified.

In one larger organizer an empty bowl for water, a small container of objects, labels for "sink" and "float," and drawing materials make the activity fairly clear. Similarly, an arrangement for working with paint might include newspaper, a sponge, and paper towels displayed together, so as to clarify preparation and cleaning procedures.

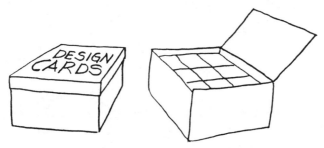

Some separately packed materials are meant to be used together.

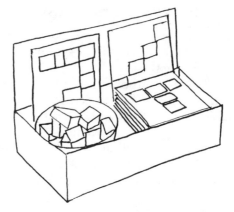

Activities are suggested when materials are combined.

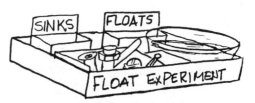

An experiment with some objects can be suggested by their display.

Newspapers, a sponge, and paper towels clarify preparation and cleanup.

Checking Your Own Environment

You can check the display and organization of materials in your learning environment by taking time to observe just how much children actually use those materials. By observing materials from one area at a time, and recording their use at regular intervals, you can see which materials are in use and which aren't.

1. Select a storage area for observation and choose several materials to watch.
2. Make a simple recording sheet like the one in the figure below that lets you record the following information quickly:
   — Is the material used, shelved, or abandoned?
   — How many children are using it right now?
   — When is it used?
3. Decide when you will observe and for how long.
4. Establish time intervals for recording, such as every ten minutes for a full day, or every five minutes for a morning.
5. Once in each interval look for the materials you are observing, and quickly record the information for each.
6. After the recording is completed, review it for this information:
   — What is the *frequency of use* (the total number of time segments in which it was used) for each material?

	CLAY	MARKERS	ABACUS	DICTIONARY	TISSUE PAPER	WORD GAME	NUMBER RODS
9:00	XI Table	Sh	I Table	Sh	Sh	IUI Table	Sh
9:15	A	I Desk	I Table	XI Desk			
9:20	I Table	II Table	IUI Floor	II Desks			
9:25	II Floor	IU Desk Table	A				
9:30	II Floor	A					
9:45	Sh						
10:00	Sh						
totals	8						

A recording sheet for materials use.

— What is the child-use-count (the total number of children using, from all time segments)?

— What material is unused?

— Are children carrying material away, or using it near the place where it is stored?

Don't be too surprised if your recorded observations differ from your prior impressions about the use of these materials. Many teachers find that, until they focus on it deliberately, they have only a vague idea about children's use of materials. The information will direct you to new ways of arranging material in your environment.

CHAPTER 7

DISTRIBUTION OF MATERIALS

Most teachers create a pattern for the placement of learning materials when they first set up the environment, and the pattern remains consistent throughout the school year. It may be a pattern of centralized storage, with all the similar provisions like pencils, scissors, or library books kept together in one location, or it may be decentralized, with similar materials separated and placed in many different locations. The pattern for materials distribution that is chosen controls the situations and times when children encounter learning materials, and so determines whether or not the materials can engage interest and stimulate learning activities.

Different patterns of materials distribution tend to generate predictable behaviors that can enhance or interfere with children's learning. Centralized patterns are associated with short attention span, interruptions, and unproductive movement. Decentralized patterns, which place materials on the basis of their role in stimulating learning rather than their similarity, are associated with long attention span, self-direction, and breadth of learning.

A Classroom with Centralized Storage

John Baca wasn't sure what was missing from the learning environment for his group of fifth graders. Many things were going very well. There was a good feeling for problem solving and for thinking together. Routines went smoothly, and the children were able to carry through with a day's work quite purposefully. They were responsible about the environment and its materials, using them appropriately and working together at the end of the day to get the classroom ready for the next morning.

149

Still, John had a sense of things that could be happening, but weren't. The students showed interest in almost any subject they encountered and responded enthusiastically to any project or topic the teacher presented. But even with encouragement they weren't initiating their own inquiry and projects. Globes, maps, and atlases were left unused except when John directed children to them, despite the group's lively interest in current events and geography. Children who were perfectly willing and quite able to use a dictionary when the teacher suggested it rarely used reference books of their own accord. Assignments and projects seemed to take longer than anyone expected, although generally the children found their work interesting and were confident of their ability to carry it out. They seemed purposeful as they went about the day's tasks, yet each afternoon there was work left to carry over into the next day.

One day John and his student teacher looked over a sketch map of the classroom, showing the materials kept in each area (see figure below). It revealed a centralized pattern of material storage in the

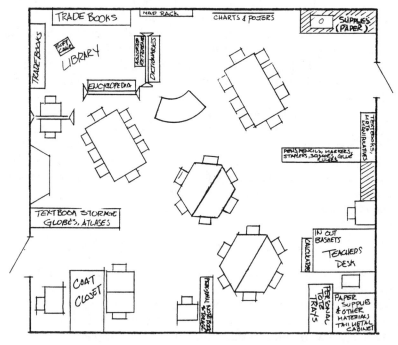

The sketch map showed centralized material storage.

environment. Books and references, except texts, were in one corner of the environment, most of them behind a screen and therefore visible only from inside the library area. Unused textbooks were stored in open bookcases, and a large collection of common tools (markers, crayons, scissors, rulers, staplers, glue, pencils) were arranged in open boxes on top of a low bookcase. Paper of several kinds was kept in a drawer near the sink, and in a closed metal cabinet in a corner across the room. All the paper was available to the students. The teacher's desk, close to the metal cabinet, held baskets for in and outgoing assignments and some special tools and materials for children's use. A small shelf held calculators and other math manipulatives. Nearby was a rack holding each child's plastic bin for personal storage, but children kept much of their work in individual notebooks all stored in a single shelf unit, so the teacher and children could have access to them.

Observations by the student teacher on the children's use of materials were revealing. A record of one morning showed that most of the children used their own personal belongings (pencils, pens, erasers, notebooks, and one pocket Spanish-English dictionary) much more than the shared materials from the environment. The most used materials from the environment were the common tools stored on the bookcase top.

Looking at the records to see how often children used information sources, John found only six instances throughout the morning. Three children used dictionaries, but two of them were sent to them by the teacher. The child who looked up the spelling of a word on his own was sitting next to the shelf holding reference books. Another child referred to a small chart that had been presented earlier in the morning and then left on her work table. A poster showing a time line with pictures of manmade dwellings from prehistoric times to the present was used as a reference by one of several boys writing about construction of dugout houses; the poster hung on a bulletin board beside his desk. In another location a girl picked up a world globe from the shelf in front of her table, running her finger over the surface as she turned the globe, until she found what she was looking for; after writing a few words in her notebook, she returned the globe to the shelf.

The teachers suddenly realized that the children were making independent use of only those tools and materials clearly visible near their working places. The collection of fiction and nonfiction trade books in the library, the calculators and abacus and other materials, the writing and drawing paper in the cabinet and drawers, the models and artifacts displayed on the lower shelf of a bookcase, the historical maps and

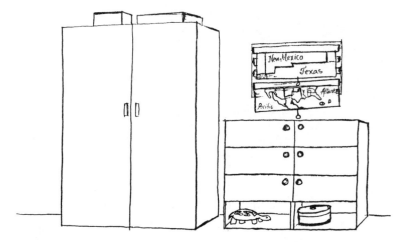

The unseen materials went unnoticed and unused.

posters hung on top of one another on a chart rack — all these went unnoticed and unused.

An additional observation, designed to watch children's movements and their interactions, showed a heavy traffic pattern in one quadrant of the environment where the most often used tools, notebooks, and personal belongings and the in and outgoing baskets were located. The routes children followed to get to these necessary locations took them past other children at work, but not past displays of information sources, raw materials, or tools other than those already in use. There was no chance for the unseen materials and equipment to stimulate interest or remind children of use possibilities as they moved about the environment.

The children's interactions during the morning were also interesting. On each trip to pick up items or return them to their storage places, almost everyone paused at least once to look at another person's work or to visit for a while. A great many of the interactions among children consisted of one person asking another for information. Children exchanged spellings, geographical locations, word meanings, and translations between Spanish and English, instead of using available information sources. The amount of time spent asking for information and gathering materials seemed to take up more time than either the work itself or the planning consultations with classmates, or making use of learned skills to locate and use specific information.

John's sense of something missing in the learning environment seemed much clearer to him after examining the observation data. A distribution of the learning materials around the environment, where

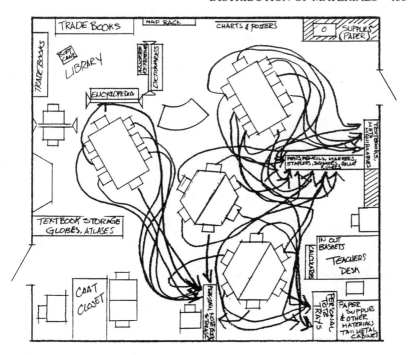

The traffic routes didn't take children near information sources.

Children asked classmates for information easily available
in references.

they could be seen and remind children of their use possibilities, would certainly enrich the environment. It would also increase the likelihood that children could initiate their own learning experiences because of interesting ideas, information, and tools provided where they would encounter them again and again.

Materials Distribution and Management

Continuous movement is a predictable effect of centralized material storage. Locating similar materials in a single location creates a pattern of movement for materials, so that children seem to be on the march all the time. They walk to pick up one item here, another over there, to carry them to yet a third place for use. Just as the hush of concentration begins to settle over the whole environment, one child walks across the room for paper, another returns to his original location with something, and a third gets up to find a reference. Others stop work to see who is passing by, interrupting their train of thought. Some of those children will return to their original focus, but others can't easily do this and need assistance from the teacher to get back to their work.

Spontaneous movement around the learning environment can be very useful for children's learning. The opportunity to notice other children's projects and approaches to work stimulates interest and new ideas. However, the problem in centralized classrooms is that the movement pattern is almost random and not productive. In a way, the movement isn't even voluntary for the learners, who might be more comfortable settling into their work and staying with it. But when environmental arrangements demand movement, children have no choice, and the environment-generated movement in turn generates disruption and distraction.

Some children who are interrupted can't get back to their work.

**Children may be caught up in social interactions and forget where
they were going or what they were doing.**

Attention spans in the classroom with centralized storage are
usually shorter than the children's actual capacity for sustained attention.
Each time a person turns away from work and moves somewhere else to
pick up needed materials, there is a strong possibility that the work will
be abandoned at least for a while. A child may become involved with
another mover or get caught up in interesting interactions and events at
other locations. It is quite possible that by the time the material is in
hand, the student will have lost track of its purpose. There are also
hazards for children who stay at work in their original places while others
are in motion: when movers pass close by, they may interrupt their work
to investigate the others' movement or interact with them.

Centralized storage of learning materials produces similar effects in
environments arranged for formal or informal programs. It's not the
amount of movement that is troublesome, but the unproductiveness of
the movement and the interference it can cause. Teachers often mistake
the events generated by centralized storage patterns for disinterest or
restlessness, but their source is in the teacher-arranged environment.
Teachers who find those behaviors unacceptable can change them in
almost the same way they were created, by a pattern of materials
distribution. Decentralizing materials usually brings marked changes.

Decentralizing Learning Materials

Once a teacher decides to decentralize materials in the environment, an initial reorganization can be done fairly quickly with gratifying
results. Decisions about the locations of materials are made on the basis
of the quantity of material, the places where it will be used, and the
number of people who need it. Traffic patterns and transitions become

smoother, traffic jams at shelf units decrease, and fewer interruptions occur.

Decentralizing materials is more than a classroom management tool. It is also a means of getting materials into the learners' hands where and when the learners need them. It means that materials within each provisioning category are separated, then distributed throughout the environment. Basic collections of the most often used tools and materials are placed in every learning area. Provisions are reorganized in new combinations and placed at locations where they can suggest and support learning activities.

To distribute materials to many different locations, teachers first subdivide the most common or versatile bulk materials such as paste, and duplicated objects like pens, into smaller quantities. Teachers can subdivide more specialized materials somewhat differently, placing small collections of similar materials in a single location while distributing the rest about the environment. A seasonal collection of trade books in a small library area doesn't have to empty the rest of the environment, if the majority of trade books and references are distributed in many areas.

Getting Materials and Work Spaces Together

A good way to arrange for students to have learning materials available when and where they need them is to organize storage furniture so that every working area is served by nearby materials readily accessible from the work space. When furniture in the environment is flexible enough to permit it, decentralizing storage units and work spaces is very useful. In environments where furniture is less flexible, shelving and

The table surface is still usable if materials are compactly arranged.

Temporary storage can be set up on one end of the table.

other kinds of display can be improvised, and work spaces can be created in the vicinity of built-in shelves.

The surface of a table is still available for work when a small collection of needed materials is compactly arranged in a divided box on the table or within reach nearby. And if storage shelves aren't plentiful, parts of tables can also display materials. A temporary shelf arrangement can be set up on one end of the table to hold learning materials, leaving the rest of the table free as a work space. Shelving can be easily created from corrugated cardboard or lumber with blocks, scrap lumber, or weighted food cans as supports. Divided cartons turned on their sides can also hold materials. In addition, deep boxes, cans, or baskets can be hung beside vertical work spaces like easels, chalkboards, and chart

Common materials can be stored beside vertical work spaces.

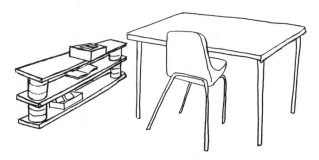

Improvised shelving keeps materials near work spaces.

racks. They can hold commonly needed materials like tape, crayons, a few pencils, paper clips, tacks, and slips of paper for labeling.

When storage units aren't available, shelving can be improvised and placed near tables or other work spaces so children have the learning materials they need for their work. Wire display stands or greeting card display racks are sometimes available from drugstores and make good material storage units. Lumber, tri-wall cardboard, or particle board shelving can be supported with bricks, sand-filled cans from the school cafeteria, or cinder blocks.

Places for work can also be decentralized. Individual tables or groups of desks can be located close to built-in storage units, each in a different area of the environment.

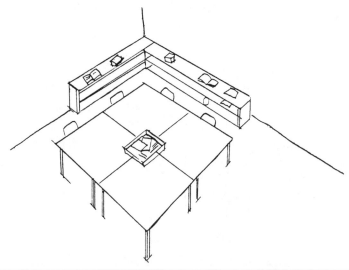

When shelving is fixed, work spaces are moved to the materials.

Smoothing Routines and Transitions

When centralized material arrangement is the pattern, congestion and crowding at storage units are common at the beginnings and ends of sessions, as everybody tries to pick up or return materials in the same place at the same time. Routines and transition times can be improved by decentralization of many materials, which helps separate personal storage containers, tools and equipment for cleanup, and other special materials many people will need at the same time. When these materials and assignment baskets are housed in several different places, congestion is reduced. If there are clear paths to their locations and room enough for the predicted number of people to get to them, transition times are much less hectic. There is the added advantage, too, that materials are more likely to survive unspilled and unbroken, and ready for the next person's use, if children aren't all jostling for access to a single storage shelf.

Personal storage bins or lockers are often needed by many children all at once. When they are all in the same area, only the people in front can get to their belongings, and it's hard for them to move away so someone else can get in, especially when others are pressing forward themselves. A few storage bins in different areas will make it easier.

Cleanup time at the end of a session or a day is faster and easier when cleaning tools are distributed throughout the environment instead of stored under the sink. Such tools, after all, are used in many different places in the environment at the same time. Similarly, since access to paper and other special supplies is often needed by many people at particular times of day, beginnings and endings of activity periods are easier and less crowded when many kinds of supplies are present in every area, rather than in a central place.

Crowding comes from putting all the personal storage bins together.

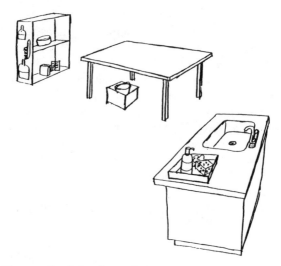

**Decentralized cleaning tools are more accessible at the end
of a session.**

**Beginnings and endings of periods are easy with all kinds of supplies
in every area.**

Distributing Materials in New Ways

Once learning materials have been separated, they can be redistributed and regrouped for reasons other than their similarity. Distributing materials on the basis of easy access and minimal interference has positive effects on self-management and routines in the environment. Combining materials in new ways, on the basis of their different contributions to the learning process, can affect learning outcomes. Juxtaposing different materials influences potential uses perceived by children, suggests that materials be used together, and also implies connections among the materials. As a result, new combinations can stimulate and support activities calling upon skills, thinking processes, and new directions of inquiry.

Grouping Diverse Materials

The qualities of a learning material that become most noticeable are determined by its surroundings. Depending on the other materials that accompany them, provisions can stimulate varied activities. Thoughtful placement of materials in different settings increases the range of suggestions they can offer.

Each kind of learning material plays a particular role in the support of learning experiences. To be most effective in suggesting activities without teacher intervention, they must be combined with other types of materials. Quantities of a single material, displayed alone, do not make very active suggestions. Information sources and some raw materials, in arrangements with other materials, are more apt to suggest ideas. Action appears when tools for processing materials are added. Further possibilities for activity are suggested with the addition of recording tools and materials, while continuation of activity is suggested by containers and labeling materials.

Combining tools, raw materials, and information sources in a single space expands the potential of each material to stimulate learning activity through the combined suggestions of all. Individual children may perceive the suggestions differently, but learning activities can be generated without teacher assignments or task cards, because combinations of diverse materials suggest them.

Sometimes materials can be combined for a specific purpose and meet that purpose, even though they generate somewhat different experiences for each child. A teacher who expects recording or writing to be part of learning activities puts recording tools and paper beside a balance arranged with a variety of small raw materials. From this combination, individual children might think of graphing, illustrating the workings of the balance, writing about their own activity, recording hypotheses and

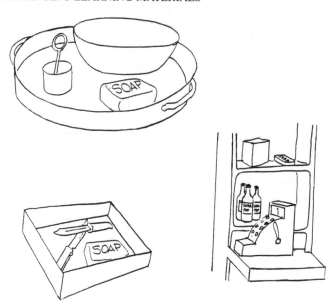

Bar soap offers different suggestions in different combinations.

data, or some other actions related to recording or writing. Whatever suggestion each child perceives in the materials, the teacher's purpose of extending the activity beyond manipulation of the balance into recording or writing has been built into the material arrangement for everybody.

A raw material like bar soap offers different suggestions in combination with different materials. With carving tools, one activity is implied, with water and a bubble pipe, another. When the bar of soap is combined with the props and other paraphernalia of a model grocery store, still different activities are suggested.

A collection of paper tubes in a holder can be well displayed and easily available, but they don't suggest any particular activity. When

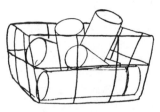

Alone, paper tubes don't suggest an activity.

Each new kind of material brings a new suggestion for activity.

glue, string, scissors, and paint are added, some actions on the paper tubes are suggested. With information sources about tube construction, new ideas and relationships among the materials are implied. Paper and recording tools suggest labeling, explaining the completed projects, or illustrating the process of construction.

Grouping Materials to Engage Interest

The knowledge content of the learning activities suggested by material groupings is provided by the information sources in each arrangement. Information sources that vividly display data can also engage children's interest in the topics and ideas they represent. Posters, living organisms, and models, if available for children to observe or examine in detail, can help them encounter and become interested in new information. When these displayed information sources are combined with reference books, pictures, and other more detailed sources on the same topics, children's specific searches for further information are encouraged. Raw materials can also engage children's interest, when arranged in combination with tools suggesting new ways to use, shape, or combine those materials. Familiar raw materials in slightly different forms and combinations can often renew children's interest in forgotten materials.

Including materials for children's labeling and display with every material grouping is an indirect but effective way to engage children's interest. When display facilities are near the material groupings, one child's displayed work can stimulate the study of another.

Large study pictures from commercial sets are interesting and offer a good deal of information. Interest generated by a study picture can be followed up with other provisions grouped nearby. A working model that invites manipulation also engages children's interest: further information searches, experimentation, and note taking can be encouraged by

Interest generated by study posters can be followed up with nearby provisions.

Working models engage interest; other materials can suggest
experimentation.

Records of growth arouse interest in plant growing.

other materials grouped with the model. Children's records of bean-plant growth, displayed near the living plants, can arouse other children's interest. Related materials displayed near the plants suggest the study of seeds and plant growth.

Distributing Material Groupings

Children need frequent reminders and opportunities each day for the practice and maintenance of a variety of developing skills and abilities. Many of the suggestions and reminders for exercising those abilities can come from combinations of materials and tools, when these are located where the children will encounter them frequently. The presence of any tool or material near a working child suggests its use, while materials at a distance are easily overlooked. Children tend to use those resources they most often see and those they can reach as they work. The children who seem to spontaneously engage in such activities as notetaking, classification, calculation, or observation of fine details probably engage in such activities because they often encounter tools, information sources, and materials related to these activities.

Some children, either by choice or by assignment, spend most of their day in one area of the environment. Their spontaneous encounters with the knowledge content and potential skills represented by learning materials are limited to those materials present in that area. An environment with centralized materials may prompt these children to use some skills again and again, but others not at all, except when the teacher reminds them.

Even when materials are separated, then regrouped in new combinations, the location of those new groups of provisions can also have a centralized or decentralized pattern. Clustering material groups together by the content represented in their information sources may also limit children's encounters with knowledge. The provisions of such an area can stimulate only a narrow range of interests. In such settings teachers find themselves initiating study topics and projects in order to engage children's interest. On the other hand, diverse groups of materials widely distributed throughout the environment can broaden the range of materials, ideas, and suggestions that children encounter, whether they stay in one location or use many areas of the environment for their work.

Material groupings located on cabinet tops, or on shelving visible from paths, help children encounter new ideas and possibilities for learning activity as they move through the environment. Sometimes extra long or extra tall shelf units can be divided into smaller sections and the sections placed in different areas. Children are apt to encounter a greater variety of material groupings and their suggestions, when the furniture to organize them is decentralized. When different content areas are represented in the material groupings located in one part of the environment, children who work in that area encounter reminders and study possibilities across the curriculum in the course of the day.

Materials visible from paths offer new ideas as children move past.

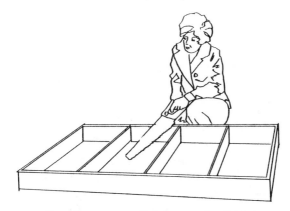

Sometimes extra tall shelves can be divided.

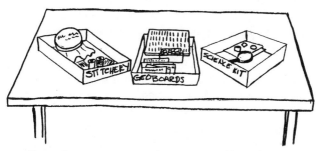

**Several content areas can be represented in each part
of the environment.**

Combining Materials for Complexity

In their studies of the learning enviornment, Kritchevsky and Prescott found that children remained involved with learning activities longer in areas provisioned with complexity. The amount of complexity in the environment's provisions affected the children's attention span, their ability to initiate learning activities, their level of involvement, and their independence in activities. Low levels of complexity were associated with short attention span, superficial involvement, and dependence on adult assistance and direction.[1]

Some materials in themselves are more complex than others and are more supportive to children's sustained interest. Most of the environment's complexity, however, comes not from the single materials in its

[1]*Sybil Kritchevsky, Elizabeth Prescott, and Lee Walling,* Planning Environments for Young Children: Physical Space, *2nd ed. (Washington, D.C.: National Association for the Education of Young Children, 1977), pp. 11–17.*

provisions, but from the particular combinations of materials arranged in the areas where students work. The complexity of a group of materials depends upon the number of different options for action they present. Complexity runs the gamut from simple materials offering few options to complex materials offering several options, and then to supercomplex collections offering a great many options for action.

Kritchevsky identifies activity units as simple, complex, and super units, in terms of the number of combined materials they offer for use. Simple units offer single use or a single material and support activity for short periods of time. A small table with hand-held mirrors on it is a simple unit, as is a classroom center set up as a fraction matching game.[2]

Complex units offer two markedly different materials, like mirrors and a book about secret codes and mirror writing. A unit like a block area, holding a single kind of material with many different subparts, is also a complex unit. Such units hold children's interest for fairly long periods of time because the addition of a different material, or the many subparts that can be combined in numerous ways, multiplies the possibilities for activity.[3]

Super units are created when complex materials are placed with another very different material, or when three or more essentially different materials are combined. Adding paper and pencil and other recording provisions to the mirrors and code book, and adding accessories such as vehicles or animal figures to the block area, change those from complex to super units. The additional materials again increase the possibilities for activity considerably, so that super units can keep children involved in learning activity for long periods of time.[4]

Complexity, or the lack of it, can have powerful effects on the general climate of the learning environment when children are at work. In environments with good spatial organization, ample provisioning, and clear materials display, children can still appear flighty and unsettled, bored, and unable to operate without considerable help from adults. An examination of the complexity of activity units and material groupings often explains such events. When these behaviors occur, it is frequently because most of the material groupings and activity units are fairly low in complexity. Even though there may be a great many simple units or material groupings, and children seem to have enough to do, the environment's contents are basically simple, so it is difficult for children to maintain active interest in their learning activities for any length of time.[5]

[2]*Ibid., p. 11.*

[3]*Ibid., p. 11.*

[4]*Ibid., pp. 11–12.*

[5]*Ibid., p. 15.*

Old magazines offer more complexity when combined with other materials.

Changing the level of complexity can help children become more self-directive and maintain their attention for longer periods of time. Fortunately, changing the level of complexity can be a matter of creating new combinations of materials already in the environment; it doesn't necessarily require bringing in additional materials.

A collection of old magazines is a good resource for a learning environment. By themselves, the magazines don't offer many things to do, but once assembled with several other materials, they offer much more complexity and can support children's interested activity. Lined and unlined paper of different sizes, construction paper and cardboard, yarn, cloth, buttons, glue, a dictionary, and display labels all multiply the possibilities.

A couple of hand-held mirrors will support children's explorations with reflections for a while. Moving a flashlight, colored cellophane, or some parquetry blocks beside the mirrors will expand the children's exploration possibilites. Complexity is further extended with recording tools and materials.

A flashlight and other objects add complexity to mirrors.

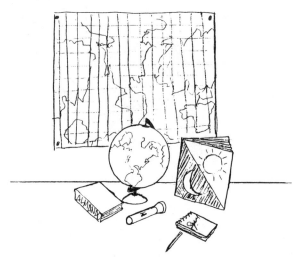

Information sources with a globe offer options for activity.

A globe of the earth can be used as a reference, but suggests few activity possibilities when alone in an area. A posted map with time zones, a flashlight, some books on day and night, an almanac, and a pamphlet on overseas telephoning can be brought together to increase the level of complexity for older children.

Checking Your Own Environment

The pattern of materials distribution in your environment can be checked by observing specific children and their use of learning materials. Observing one child at a time, you can see how well the environment supports continuous encounters and involvement with learning materials. Observe the child at regular intervals to see the materials, activity, and location of that activity. For a half-day session, a five-minute interval is useful; for a full day, every ten minutes will do.

1. Choose the child you will observe and select the time intervals.
2. Prepare a simple recording sheet like the one on page 171 to receive the following information quickly:
   — What materials are in the child's hand or nearby?
   — Where is the material usually stored?
   — What activity is the child engaged in?
   — Where is the child located?
   — Does the child have direct access to material or must the material be given by the teacher?

Richard S.   Feb. 26

Time:	9:10	9:15
Material:	wood, hammer, nails	Same
Activity:	building airplane	Same
Location:	workbench	Same
Access or Given:	access	same
When Stored:	at workbench	same
Time:	9:20	9:25
Material:	sandpaper, sanding block	Sanding block, plane
Activity:	fastens sandpaper to block	Sandpapering plane
Location:	workbench	workbench
Access or Given:	access	access
Where Stored:	at workbench	at workbench
Time:	9:30	
Material:	Broom	
Activity	Sweeping	
Location	Carpentry area	

A recording sheet for children's use of materials.

3. Once during each time interval, observe the child and record the information on the record sheet.
4. After the recordings are completed, review the data for this information:
   — How many different kinds of material or equipment does the child use during your observation?

— How much repetition or revisiting of materials is evident? What provisioning categories are involved?

— Does the child travel to get material? Were the used materials encountered in his movements? Were the used materials arranged close to the child's working place?

— How does the range of materials used by this child compare with the range of materials available in the environment?

Observing one child gives you some interesting information about the learning opportunities encountered and used. Information from the observations of several children will show you how well the material distribution pattern is supporting the children's continuous involvement in learning. Combining the information from these observations with a record of traffic patterns will help you assess the extent to which material distribution may be influencing children's movement in the environment.

SECTION IV

ORGANIZING FOR SPECIAL PURPOSES

CHAPTER 8

PROMOTING LITERACY

Children gradually develop competence in literacy through countless experiences with literate behaviors and skills. In classrooms for developing readers and children not yet reading, reflections of literacy in the environment encourage the use of language and literacy skills and establish the need to develop more. Literate surroundings can give meaning to print by associating it with the events, people, and materials encountered by children in the environment. Reflections of literacy help children move into the world of literature through frequent and satisfying encounters with books.

If I Didn't Make Them, They'd Never Write

Maggie Bailey and Bertha Chin, who taught in adjoining classrooms, often exchanged comments about their children. "I don't understand it," Maggie said one day. "Your kids seem to be writing all the time. Every time I look over, I see somebody looking for a place to hang up something they've written. In my room the children aren't interested in writing at all."

She looked at the deserted Creative Writing Center in her own classroom and sighed. Two small carrels were arranged on a table, each containing a box of file cards labeled "Story Starters," a few sheets of lined writing paper, and an empty can labeled "Pencils." Some teachermade signs inside the carrels said "Writing Stories is Fun!" and "Can You Think of a Good Story?" Someone had taken the chairs away during the day.

Maggie had set up the center as a place where children could write their own stories about topics of their choice. She hoped it would spark

The Creative Writing Center was deserted.

interest in other kinds of writing, too. For the first few days everybody wanted to use the center, but then children began to ignore it. They used the materials for other purposes. It seemed to the teacher that the children had no interest in writing.

"Maybe they don't use the center because there are other places to write," suggested Bertha. "I found that a writing center was almost ignored in my room, because there were quite a few other places with tools for writing and things to write about." Maggie was sure plenty of writing tools were available in her room, too. Markers, crayons, extra pencils, and some felt pens were all stored in a cabinet beside the teacher's desk. The same cabinet held all the writing, drawing, graph, chart, and construction paper, as well as scissors, glue, staplers, thumbtacks, and other classroom tools. Anyone who needed supplies was free to open the cabinet and take them. Children kept their own personal writing tools and notebooks with them at their work tables.

Bertha observed that the children wrote more when they could use the bulletin boards to post their own writing. She reserved the lower

Writing tools were all stored inside the cabinet.

The students could post their own writing.

sections of bulletin boards, within children's reach, for their own display. The tops of the boards were saved for teacher use. "Almost everyone began to write more," she said, "when I put some word lists on bulletin boards and spread the dictionaries around, too."

Maggie thought about using the bulletin boards in the same way, but there wasn't enough display space to spare. She used the boards to display children's work in complete sets, so no child was left out. In her classroom the bulletin boards were filled with three sets of stories, one entitled Monsters and the others on seasonal topics. Every child had written and illustrated a few lines for each display.

As they looked over the displayed sets of stories, Bertha said, "But your children can do some very nice writing, Maggie. Most of these stories are well written."

"Yes, I know they are," said Maggie. "Some of them can produce delightful stories. I insist on good work when I give them their weekly writing assignment. But if I didn't make them, they'd never write at all!"

Arranging for Reading and Writing

The major difference between Miss Chin's environment, where children wrote spontaneously, and Mrs. Bailey's, where they seemed disinterested, was that Miss Chin's provided easy access to tools and materials for reading and writing, spaces for using those tools and materials, and something interesting to read and write about. The visible presence of these provisions and the way they were arranged within the environment were equally important.

The widespread distribution of tools and materials in Bertha Chin's classroom offered constant encounters with print and continuous stimulus for writing. Markers, pencils, paper, and other writing materials were present when and wherever any child might notice something to record. Even though the presence of appropriate tools and materials didn't guarantee immediate writing by every child, the opportunity was given, and children usually responded in some way. Without built-in reminders and opportunity, children aren't likely to record events and ideas spontaneously.

Every area of a learning environment can have a small, visibly arranged collection of writing and drawing tools and varieties of paper for recording with words or illustration. References like word lists, books, and diagrams extend activity possibilities to the search for further information. Even though the particular activities or specialized materials designated for each area are different, similar assortments of common materials and tools can provide the stimulus and opportunity for

Mrs. Bailey   Miss Chin

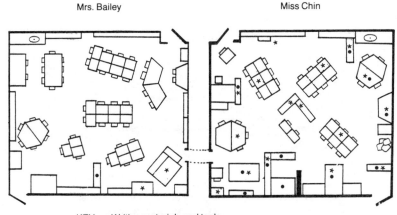

KEY   ∗ Writing materials and tools
      • References (dictionary, encyclopedia, word list, chart)

One room had writing tools in one place, but the other displayed them everywhere.

recording. The reference materials in an area are most useful when related to the specialized purpose of the area or to other materials arranged there.

Opportunities for Recording

Whatever the activity in progress, a small collection of common tools and materials beside every work space can suggest planning and recording events, or labeling an individual's work. Blank labels of several sizes and recording tools located near the work spaces encourage written identification and explanation that children can dictate or write.

Suggestions to seek and make note of information from print, graphs, diagrams, or other symbolic material can be arranged anywhere, by making sure that references are accompanied by paper and tools for

Writing tools suggest writing or labeling.

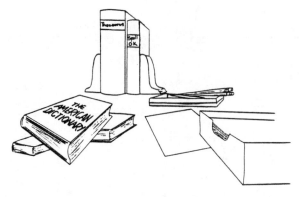

Suggestions to make notes can be arranged anywhere.

writing notes. Some record keeping is also needed to maintain adequate provisioning; arranging recording sheets and writing tools in appropriate areas helps children collect the information. And experiments and their results likewise call for record keeping to verify methods and findings.

References Where They Are Needed

A list of often requested words makes a helpful reference for those children who want to write signs and stories about their creations. A map

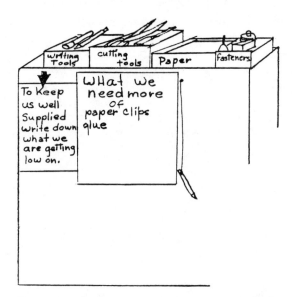

Record-keeping tools help children collect information.

Experiments and their results call for record keeping.

of the area where the children live is interesting; it can attract them to print information nearby. And the encyclopedia becomes even more important when removed from the reference shelf and distributed around the environment for a short time. During a windy season the K volume could be placed near tissue paper, wood strips, string, and books on kites.

Word lists make helpful references.

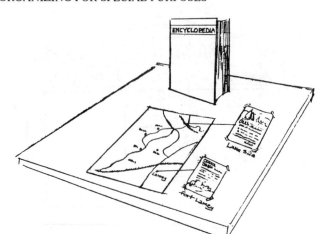

A map of familiar territory leads to related print information.

An encyclopedia is useful when located near materials.

Places to Research and Write

Surfaces for writing and space for settling down to use the references and materials can be arranged in each area of the environment. These lend further support to the suggestions to record and seek useful information from books, diagrams, and other references. When materials are carefully distributed and tools are arranged close to work spaces, suggestions for spontaneous writing and reading can be followed easily.

What did you see outside?

4 blue birds
5 Cats

Vertical surfaces provide places to write.

Vertical surfaces like the sides of cabinets can provide places to write when paper and writing tools are attached. Sometimes a person needs a place to write in alone; clipboards can offer writing surfaces in areas without table space.

Some children are comfortable at very low tables, when low shelf units in the area offer related references, materials, and tools. Occasionally the top of a shelf unit is a good place for writing.

Things to Talk, Read, and Write About

Children are most likely to use their developing literacy skills when they find interesting things to read and write about in the environment. Print and nonprint information sources can offer stimulating content in each area. Objects and living things, and reminders of events and things seen elsewhere, offer purpose for reading and writing. Animals, models, artifacts, machines, and other realia are interesting to watch, manipulate, examine, and read about if the tools for doing so are present. Photographs, stories, souvenirs, and variants of familiar objects all serve as reminders of previous experiences. These offer reasons to read more, to record those previous experiences, or to share information about them with others. The spontaneous reading activities and writings of children

Sometimes a person needs a place to write in alone.

are as varied in substance as the children and their interests, when they are stimulated by a variety of information sources, tools, and work spaces.

Simple machines and their actions invite manipulation, speculation, and a reason to read more and perhaps to record observations. Children can also share, examine, and research insects and cocoons in references that "happen" to be nearby. Combining related print and nonprint information sources on the topic in the right season gives a good stimulus to find more details from print. Twenty-year-old photographs of

Children can write at low tables or on tops of shelves.

Simple machines invite reading and recording.

the community look a little different from today's pictures; children can read about the community, compare and note specific differences, and report explanations gathered from older residents. And children's models and constructions, stimulated by interesting raw materials, also offer good reasons to write stories or make records of plans and construction methods.

Putting nonprint with print information sources encourages reading.

Old photographs of the community lead to reading.

Constructions offer content for records of plans and methods.

Displaying the Written Word

There are two major reasons to display the written word in the learning environment. One is to provide opportunities for children to read symbols and print. This requires a readable display that must be perceptually clear, so children can see and distinguish elements of the writing fairly easily. The other reason is to develop awareness of writing as a medium for expression, communication, and pleasure. This calls for a large quantity of written material in appreciative displays at any given time. Each child knows his writings are appreciated when he sees them displayed for others to enjoy.

The perceptual clarity of print, like clarity in display of learning materials, requires an empty background with space between displayed items, in preference to quantity and a crowded display. This may seem to imply that arrangements for readable display and for appreciative display of quantities of writing are in conflict, but it is possible to arrange for both kinds of display, although they won't occur in precisely the same spaces.

Appreciative Display

Gallerylike display arrangments can be created along the backs or sides of some cabinets, on folding screens that divide space, on tackstrips near coat closets and doorways, or above chalkboards. Areas like

Gallerylike display arrangements can be created.

The triangle house was on the hill. Many steps came up to the door.

Child-written materials can be combined in book form.

these, where children pass by but don't stay for work activity, are useful for the quantity display of children's writing. It's likely that some of this material will go unread, as it often does in a crowded, perceptually unclear display on lower or more centrally located bulletin boards. However, writers will know their work is on display and appreciated, and others will know that their classmates have created stories, illustrations, or reports. Collections of child-written materials can also be combined in book form, which offers easier access and more legibility than crowded displays, and also the knowledge that each child's work is appreciated. There can be room for all children to see their work in some appreciative display arrangement, provided that materials are dated and frequent changes are encouraged by materials for new postings in the display areas.

Readable Display

The materials intended for readable display, whether written by children or adults, will be of interest when posted in all areas where learning activities are going on; some will be useful in a central place where everyone goes for information. To be readable, posted material must be visible and displayed at children's eye level or lower.

Marking permanently designated portions of display areas for single bulletins or messages makes empty space available around segments of print. Large pieces of solid color paper or framelike outlines can define each posting place. Some variation in size and shape of the designated areas helps provide for different writings, from brief mes-

Readable display is visible at the child's eye level.

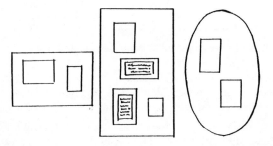

Permanent areas on bulletin boards show where to put notices.

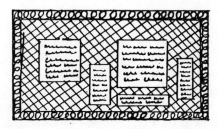

Patterned backgrounds tend to overpower print.

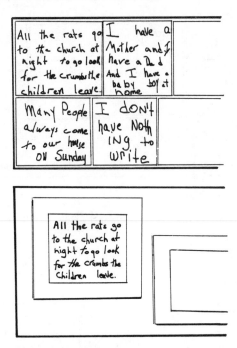

Legibility is enhanced by enlarging the area around print.

sages to reports and stories. Patterned backgrounds aren't helpful for displaying print because the design tends to overpower the print. However, the legibility of materials written by beginners can be enhanced by enlarging the empty area around the print. Children can mount their own work on oversized backings before posting. In some areas they can be encouraged to write on the right-sized paper to fit a given space by placement of the paper very close to the designated space.

Keeping Print Current

When display space seems to be at a premium, it's necessary to encourage short-term occupation of display spaces. Writings can be saved for later use or retrieved by their authors. Accurate dating of each piece of work is encouraged by the presence of calendars in every area. A container nearby to receive the outdated items removed from display keeps them from getting lost. Tacks or tape can also be placed beside the posting surface, along with the basic collection of materials and tools for recording that are already there. These materials encourage continual display of the written word and help keep posted information current, perceptually clear, and of interest to everyone.

JANUARY 1981

Sun	Mon	Tue	Wed	Thur	Fri	Sat
				1	2	3
4	5	6	7	8	9	10
11	12	13	14	15	16	17
18	19	⓴	21	22	23	24
25	26	27	28	29	30	31

Today's Notice

Tuesday
The high school band will play in the lunch room at 2:00PM

Pencil

TACK

old Notices

Paper

Yesterday's notices can be replaced with current information.

The Functional Use of Print

The routines of the school day offer many occasions for the functional use of literacy. When information needed for work in the environment is made public by posting it in written form, children need to read that print. Posted written information, in combination with other visual symbols or with materials, accommodates the many different levels of skill development within any group of children. Through the combined forms, the nonprint information helps give meaning to the print, making information available to early readers and nonreaders as well as those who read fluently.

Creating a need for literacy skills in the environment isn't difficult, but it does require thoughtful arrangement. The teacher offers short-term information in written form that could just as easily be given orally and then may arrange tools and materials so children are encouraged to do the same. Except for some labels and reminders of standing procedures, functional print isn't very important unless current. The distribution of writing and recording tools, display facilities, sentence strips, label slips, chart paper, and calendars around the environment makes it easy for children and teacher to remove the dated schedules, notices, news, and plans after one or two days, and to replace them quickly with more current information. Keeping posted information current also helps keep the information legible, since outdated information won't be left to consume space needed for the clear display of written messages.

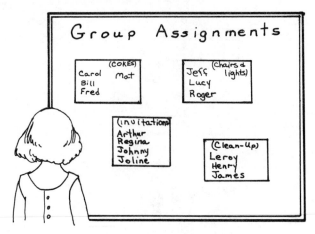

Notices give information about the day.

Posting Essential Information

Children acquire daily information about routines, procedures, and schedules through posted information. Special news and events can be announced in print where all can see it, and volunteers can commit themselves to special responsibilities in writing with the help of posted sign-up sheets. In addition, caring for special equipment becomes easy when the needed information appears right where the equipment will be used.

Special news and information can be announced in print.

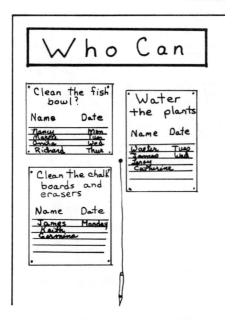

Volunteers can commit themselves in writing.

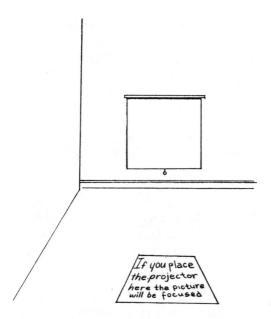

Caring for special equipment requires information.

Information can be developed and shared in writing.

Communicating and Sharing in Writing

Shared written communication within the learning environment takes many forms and can be contributed by teachers and children alike. Announcements about coming events, procedures for special activities or the care of equipment, where to find interesting materials, explanations of pictures or other art pieces, and reports can all be shared through posted print.

Information researched in many different ways can be developed and shared in writing; thus sharing the process of gathering interesting information leads to shared effort in writing it for others. Personal news can also be shared with enthusiasm when the means are readily available, and one child's work can help another get started, if words accompany the displayed work. A piece of art work can be displayed with a brief statement from the artist, when writing materials are near the display space.

Recording hypotheses and predictions is interesting when the subject is near a paper that invites guesses; people can stop by at any time to add new predictions. Class members can also call attention to sights and events when materials, tools, and display spaces encourage it. The world outside the classroom offers interesting content in the environment.

Labeling

Labeling is a special form of functional print that sometimes is short-term and sometimes remains in the environment. The teacher

Personal news can be shared with others.

offers labels in connection with learning materials and exhibited information sources in the environment. Labels don't substitute for visibility of the learning materials they identify, but in combination with materials they help children increase their understanding of print. When labels are written in phrases or sentences, such as "These magazines can be used

One child's words can help another get started.

Paper and tools invite the recording of hypotheses.

for cutting Christmas pictures,'' children use reading behaviors more like those in other reading situations than when labels are single words.

Children's labeling is sometimes related to the identification of learning materials, and even more often is connected with the display of their own work. Art work, constructions, special exhibits, and models can be enhanced by written labels that name, explain, share a process, or identify the artist or builder. Extensive labeling appears spontaneously

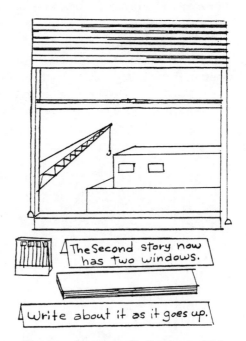

Class members can call attention to sights.

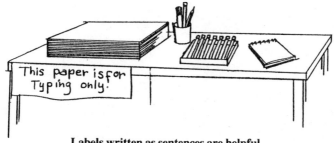

Labels written as sentences are helpful.

only when tools, materials, and empty display spaces are arranged to encourage this activity.

Labels written as sentences are helpful, for they identify objects and materials and allow children to use their developing skills. Labeling clearly visible materials helps early readers understand what the labels say. Some labels both identify the materials available and tell how and why the materials should be used.

Young children are themselves encouraged to make simple labels for constructions when blocks are accompanied by markers and large file cards. Room to display personal collections encourages children to write labels; label slips, writing tools, and references let them follow the suggestion to clarify a display with writing. Partly finished work can be placed in a waiting container where it will be ready to be continued tomorrow; children can then write labels to preserve and identify the work in progress.

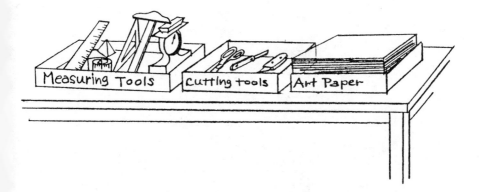

Labeling visible materials helps early readers understand what the labels say.

Labels can both identify materials and tell how and why materials should be used.

Literature Experiences

Children become enthusiastic about literature when environmental arrangements offer familiar favorites and other inviting books everywhere. Displays of literature can keep pace with children's varied activities and interests and reflect events in the community, if books are frequently changed or added to small collections in many areas. Rearranging books already in the environment, changing collections from school or public libraries, or exchanging collections with other teachers

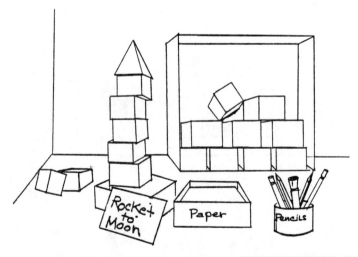

Young children can label constructions with nearby materials.

Room to display collections encourages labeling.

are ways to keep the invitations to literature fresh and to enrich the literary experiences available for children.

Most trade books published for children have beautiful cover illustrations and title print, suggesting intriguing contents. Many are illustrated extensively and invite picture browsing as well as reading. As a result, most children who see books are eager to handle and read them. Just getting books out of the library corner and located around the environment, with cover illustrations and titles showing, can increase children's awareness and use of literature.

When all the children's books are in the library corner, they are visible only to those who are in the library or close to it; for the other students the books might as well not be there, because they can't be seen. But a few books can be well displayed in each area of the environment and still leave room for other materials. In fact, the other materials can

Children can label and store partly finished work.

If all books are in the library corner, only people nearby can see them.

A few books can be well displayed in each area.

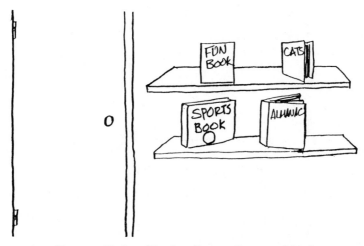

Face-out display of books calls attention to each book.

call attention to the books, if they are in some way connected to their contents.

Face-out display of books limits the number that can be fitted on a given shelf. But showing the faces of books also calls attention to each book and increases children's uses of the books. Browsing through groups of books is another way to enjoy them. Face-out display, easy physical access, and room to pause comfortably help children to sample contents with pleasure.

Browsing through books is another way to enjoy them.

Seasonal events can be reflected in book groupings.

Highlighting Books

Children can be helped to notice contents of special interest by the way books are displayed. In some areas special books can be highlighted, displayed open to an illustration or other contents that seem to match the children's interests. Books can also be placed beside other materials related to their contents. Combinations like this help children seek specific information or revisit their own experiences through stories of similar experiences by others.

Seasonal events can be reflected with groups of books, displayed to emphasize seasons or traditional and contemporary holidays. Children's illustrations of favorite books can be used to share literature experiences and to highlight the books themselves. Another child's recommendation may bring children to books they wouldn't have noticed. And very

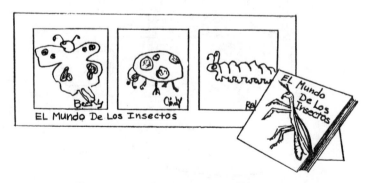

Illustrations of favorites can highlight books.

Special books can be highlighted by a lazy susan or by fabric.

special books can be displayed against a background of fabric, plain color, or textured paper; a lazy susan especially features a book with unusual illustrations and cover design.

Some books are best enjoyed with friends. Two or three children can read to one another or look at illustrations and talk them over. But listening to adults read aloud is also an enjoyable experience at any age. Space that lets a group be comfortable, yet close, increases this enjoyment.

Creating Literature

Children's experiences with the literature created for them by adults can be extended by opportunities to create their own stories, captured on

Some books are best enjoyed with a friend.

Space for a group to listen makes a pleasant book experience.

paper or in book form by writing or dictation. The presence of blank books, drawing and writing paper, simple bookbinding materials, and appropriate tools supports children's creative writing. When these are arranged close to other books, the materials can encourage the children to develop their own stories. They can also invite the children to make their own books, which will become a part of the literature of the environment.

Finding the right words to tell the story, arranging illustrations and print on a page, and preparing a story so others can read it, are all encouraged by the models offered in children's books and child-made books. Story starters come from the environment and its materials. Objects and literature present in the environment, or objects once seen and now remembered, trigger associations with past experiences and with new ideas or different views of familiar events.

Checking Your Own Environment

You can check the potential of your environment to support literacy by surveying the arrangements of materials and information. A clear assessment of literacy indicators needs an area-by-area survey to determine both their quantity and their distribution throughout the environment. This survey can be made when children are out of the environ-

The right materials can encourage and support story writing.

ment, or it can be done with their help. You may want to survey one or two areas each day until all the environment has been examined.

1. Sit in the area you intend to survey, so that you can see the environment as the children see it. (Or ask the children to look and count for you.) Look carefully around the area and count the actual number of the following literacy indicators:
   — How many posted *current* messages about the classroom day?
   — How many child-written messages, labels, or compositions that are *less than five days old?*
   — How many *clear and legible* notices, written statements, and labels?
   — How many labels or written statements *combined with pictures, objects, or materials?*
   — How many *different kinds of tools* for recording, illustrating, and writing?
   — How many *different kinds of material and equipment* to record upon?
   — How many *empty* places available for children to post records or written messages?
   — How many books, pictures, charts, and other information sources for use as references?

Place	Art/carpentry Areas	Game and Meeting Area	Sink Area	Small Group Area			
# Current Messages	3						
# Ch. Written Messages	2						
# Clear, Legible Writings	3						
# Writings with Pic, Obj., Mat'ls	9						
# Different Recording Tools	5						
# Different Recording material	3						
# Empty Display Places	3						
# References	1						
# Diff. Kinds of books	1						
# Book covers Displayed	0						
# Books Related to Materials	1						
# Other	27						
# Reflections of literacy (total)							

A record sheet for a literacy assessment.

— How many *different kinds* of books directly available to children (references, trade books, child-made and class-made books)?

— How many books *displayed* with covers showing or opened to a particular page?

— How many books *related to other materials* in the same area?

2. Make a record sheet like the one on the facing page to record the information.

3. After surveying the areas one by one, look over all the recorded information to determine:

— Is there any area a child might work in without seeing any opportunity or need for literacy?

— Are there opportunities for a variety of approaches to literacy and levels of competence in each area?

— Does each area provide multiple stimuli for the interpretation of symbols and print, for recording in symbols or print, for communication with others, and for involvement in books?

Don't be discouraged if surveys of your environment at first show a need for more reflections of literacy. Much of this can be accomplished by rearranging materials already in the environment. Keeping the posted print current and short-term will add a great deal to the environment's support of literacy. These changes aren't complex and make a good beginning at increasing reflections of literacy and supporting children's growing competence in these behaviors.

CHAPTER 9

SUPPORTING CHILDREN WITH SPECIAL NEEDS

Children with special needs who come to the regular classroom for their learning experiences are affected by environmental arrangements just as their classmates are. Environmental organization can enhance or hinder their ability to function well and make use of their strengths for learning. Spatial organization, provisioning, and materials arrangement all have positive or negative effects on learning experiences, depending on the appropriateness of environmental arrangements for children's characteristics and needs.

The environment can support children with special needs in several ways. Spatial organization and materials arrangement can be purposefully developed to give children with physical limitations access to space and materials. Provisioning can be developed to meet a variety of needs and functioning levels. Such arrangements, designed to help children make full use of their competencies, support children's growth toward independence and self-direction. The environment can be arranged to stimulate practice of skills and to offer extensions of content and knowledge in forms each child can receive. The same arrangements can also reinforce and reflect the teachers' efforts in more direct work with individuals. In this way, environmental arrangements build consistency between teacher demands and environmental suggestions for behavior and performance.

The New Children Are Coming

When the teachers first heard about the plan to place children with special needs in all the classrooms in their elementary school, they were very upset. They couldn't see how the new children could possibly fit in.

The teachers saw children function on their own.

The teachers were sure they would be spending so much time taking care of special needs that there would be little time for other children. How could the children with special needs manage in the regular classroom? How could handicapped children adapt to the routines and the teacher expectations for the class? If the new children were intellectually different from their classmates, how could they work in regular classrooms?

A few days later the teachers accepted invitations to visit a nearby elementary school where the children with special needs were integrated into the classrooms with other children. After the visit, the teachers had many experiences and much information to exchange. What they had seen and learned from the host teachers helped them prepare for the new children.

Two teachers described their observations of one classroom. When the morning was over, they realized they hadn't been especially aware of the children with special needs until the host teacher identified them. A child with vision problems was working with a classmate on a mathematics puzzle, using an abacus and recording calculations on a piece of large chart paper. Earlier the visitors had watched the same child go to a materials shelf, pick up a large basket containing the abacus, crayons, markers, and a roll of chart paper, and carry it over to the low table where the classmate waited. Watching the child gather up the materials in the basket and put it back in its place on the shelf, the visitors didn't see any actions that obviously marked a handicap. They watched the child walk along a path to the shelf, touching the shelf edge with one hand, then stop and slip the basket into the empty space on the shelf. Later the host teacher pointed out how materials were arranged on shelves without any stacking or crowding. All the materials were organized inside boxes or baskets, and there were spaces between the material holders on the shelves. Everyone in the environment could find things easily and get them back to the appropriate places at cleanup time.

Other visiting teachers shared similar experiences, observing children with special needs functioning comfortably with their classmates. They observed a child in a wheelchair who was able to enter every space in the environment to participate with classmates in their activities. A child who was exceptionally small wasn't very noticeable in the flow of activity in an environment that offered different kinds of work spaces at different heights. They noticed a child with a walker put the handle of a box of materials over one arm to carry it to a work space. They also saw a mentally retarded child sharing and discussing a construction activity with some classmates, building with tinkertoys as the other children worked on a scale model. All the builders exchanged ideas and progress reports about the constructions as they worked.

Most of the rooms observed differed little from many other elementary classrooms in arrangement. They were all arranged without

Work with classmates is difficult without many different work spaces.

uniform seating, and none contained rows or clusters of tables. The teachers talked about the barriers that could be removed for children with special needs by avoiding extremely traditional arrangements of work spaces. The wheelchair child couldn't have moved through aisles between rows of desks or joined other children at a table, and so would have been denied the chance to participate in spontaneous learning activities with classmates. With uniform seating, the exceptionally small child would have struggled each time there was a need to enter or leave a work space, or would have been the only child whose work space was different; work with classmates would have been difficult.

Materials arrangement and provisioning had also been used to remove barriers in the classrooms observed by the teachers. Describing the major differences between these and other elementary classrooms, they agreed that it was the strong sense of order and care in the display and variation of materials. All children weren't required to use exactly the same provisions.

The extent of the variation in the learning materials within each environment was a surprise for most of the teachers. As they talked it over, they could see how the variety had allowed a mentally retarded child to share an interest and an activity with classmates. At the same time and place, the more advanced children could enjoy sharing without having to work in the same way or with the same materials. The teachers noticed how barriers to information had been removed by providing nonvisual information sources for children who had visual handicaps and nonprint information sources for nonreaders, without also removing the print and other visual information sources.

Rather than reducing the amount and variety of learning materials, or simplifying their level to meet children's handicaps, the host teachers had removed barriers for children with special needs by increasing the variation of materials, which also expanded learning possibilities for all the children. The materials arrangement had been simplified so as to reduce visual confusion and facilitate access and care of materials. A less careful materials display would have prevented the visually handicapped child from finding needed materials except through dependence on others. The child in the walker might have seen and selected materials, but wouldn't have had access to them without help. Wheelchair children might not have had access to materials on lower shelves and others might have been denied those stored higher, if similar materials hadn't been stored on several levels.

After a good discussion of their observations of the integrated classrooms, the teachers were more optimistic about preparing for the new children who would be enrolling in their classrooms. Until they knew more about the specific children and their special needs, the

Materials arrangement helps children with visual or coordination problems.

teachers would examine their own environments for potential barriers to children like those they had observed. Some general planning and reorganizing of materials and space would improve the environments for the children now there. The teachers would begin to increase the variety of learning materials through trading, and would develop clearer material organizaton. Then, when the needs of individual children were known, special arrangements would result in an environment with relatively few barriers and a great deal of support for the children with special needs.

Environmental Barriers and Supports

The environmental tasks of spatial organization, provisioning, and materials arrangement all influence events within the environment in particular ways. They can create problems for children with special needs, or they can help them function in the environment and participate comfortably in learning activities. Children with handicaps can negotiate the environment and the day's routines when those environmental tasks are carried out with the needs of individuals in mind, and when they reflect planned work of the teacher with children. Through this reflection, instruction can be extended into those portions of the day when children with special needs and their classmates have direct access to carefully selected materials in an environment arranged to meet their needs.

Spatial Organization

The organization of space has both direct and indirect effects in special children's learning activities. Paths organized for movement from place to place can give access to all the environment's spaces and the provisions they contain. But paths can also keep children with special needs from those spaces and provisions, if the paths fail to offer enough space for movement, so that children intrude into activity units or collide with furniture. Paths not defined clearly enough for children to perceive them where the teacher sees them can also prevent access. The ability to get to the environment's spaces and provisions determines how much children can benefit from the suggestions of learning materials and become self-directive for part of their learning.

The arrangement of work spaces and activity units can offer shelter from intrusion or generate interference, affecting special children's ability to focus attention and effort. The size and placement of those spaces limit or encourage the handling of some materials and equipment more than others, depending on whether or not there is room to spread out and manipulate materials, and a firm surface to hold materials steady. The size of work spaces controls the number of children who can fit into an area together, with potential development of language and cooperative social skills through peer interaction.

When spatial organization is harmonious with teacher expectations, children receive consistent and reinforcing messages about behavior limits and appropriate possibilities for action. The confidence with which children with special needs can negotiate the environment and the processes of learning depends on how much spatial organization supports or contradicts teachers' expectations, students' intentions, and the exercise of those competencies that children bring to their learning.

Physical access to spaces and provisions supports self-direction.

Provisioning for Learning

For several reasons, provisioning is an important part of supporting children with special needs. For all learners, the provisions of the environment determine what learning activities are possible. Depending on the materials and information offered, and the tools available to act upon them, provisions shape the form and content of learning activities. They elicit skills and processes, engage special children's attention, and provide the information from which knowledge and concepts are constructed.

Teachers make provisioning decisions for groups of children and for individuals within each group as they choose the specific tools and materials to be made directly available in the environment. With these decisions teachers can make it possible for the environment's provisions to promote or prevent learning for children with special needs. The frequent use of tools and information sources that elicit particular skills determine whether or not children can practice learned skills and acquire more. Tools and information sources can promote skill use only if they fit into the child's competencies and don't demand abilities such as grasp, vision, or body posture that aren't presently available to the child.

Although it is important to provide materials and equipment that don't exceed children's physical limitations, this doesn't mean that the variety of learning materials must be limited in an environment that includes children with special needs. Not all children in that environment have the same limitations, or for that matter the same strengths. For any group of children, a wide range of provisions is more likely to meet individuals at their own level of development and learning than a re-

Provisions that don't demand unavailable abilities help children function.

stricted range, and when special children are also present, diversity in provisioning is essential. All the children benefit by encountering a variety of specific objects and materials in each provisioning category, because they foster more learning possibilities than quantities of similar materials. Many forms of information sources, for example, can offer data about the same topic. A variety of print forms in simple and complex language, with many details or a few generalizing statements, presented in a variety of print styles on posters or charts or in books, pamphlets, or projected film, can meet the abilities of many different individuals. Nonprint information sources can offer data in tactile and aural as well as visual form.

Materials Arrangement

The way learning materials are displayed determines whether children will be aware of them and can find, reach, and return them after use. The location of materials influences how often children will interrupt work to go after materials, and at the same time determines the ideas and connections among materials that children can perceive.

Materials arrangement can prohibit physical access to materials, create visual confusion and traffic problems, and prevent children with special needs from receiving suggestions from those materials. On the other hand, purposeful display and distribution can contribute significantly to learning for all children. Materials can be arranged to offer maximum visual information, and so meet some of the needs of children with hearing disabilities. Perceptual clarity in the display of materials can reduce unfocused stimuli for children with perceptual problems. Careful spacing in display helps children with visual problems to locate materials, and facilitates consistent placement when materials are returned. Locating diverse collections of materials in every area supports the child with limited mobility in finding materials and suggestions to support ongoing learning in many different subject areas, no matter where the child is located. Storing similar materials on different shelf levels provides access for children with reach limitations. A variety of carefully designed carriers helps children with uncertain coordination move materials from one place to another when needed.

The same principles that guide material arrangement in any environment help teachers arrange materials to facilitate access and learning for children with special needs. Materials are placed with consideration for children's eye level and reach. Materials are also placed in focus through perceptually clear display, in locations where they are available for the children who need them at the times when they are needed.

Special Arrangements for Special Needs

Within the general framework of environmental organization there are many specific arrangements of space, provisioning, and material display and distribution that can help the special child participate in appropriate learning experiences. Arrangements that are necessary for special children are also effective for other children, so such arrangements can be made within the context of environmental organization for all the students. When the characteristics and needs of the individual children have been identified, it is not difficult to plan the environmental conditions that will help them function comfortably. Many arrangements that meet one set of special needs will also meet others at the same time. Careful arrangements for special children tend to expand, rather than limit, the environment's possibilities and enhance support for everybody's learning.

Organizing for Physical Problems

Spatial organization can offer considerable support for children with mobility problems, whether they require apparatus like wheelchairs, walkers, or crutches or are unsteady as they move about on their own. Spaces within activity units can be made large enough for the apparatus and whatever additional surrounding space is needed while using the unit. The width of paths can be adjusted, with special attention to corners and entrances to units. If reaching is a problem, material placement at several different levels and in a variety of locations helps meet everybody's needs. Careful material arrangement can help children with grasp or coordination problems obtain and replace materials. Holders and organizers designed for their needs facilitate this.

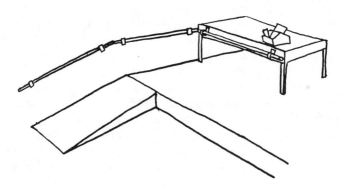

Handholds can support unsteady movement.

A variety of heights lets everyone find a place to work.

When paths are defined by the sides or backs of furniture, railings or handholds can support children with unsteady movement. Work spaces at a variety of heights, so they can be used by children on the floor, in chairs, standing, or in wheelchairs, let everyone find a place for work. Portable work spaces like lap desks, carpet squares, and cushions further support children with a variety of needs, as they look for suitable working places.

Narrow shelving keeps materials accessible for children with reach limitations. On deeper shelves, placement of materials toward the front is encouraged by attaching a strip of molding to the shelf surface. Shelving materials at different levels lets children with different reaching abilities have access to all kinds of provisions. Material holders that are light in weight and quite a bit larger than the materials help children with grasp or coordination problems. Large handles that can be hung over an arm or a shoulder are helpful, especially when holders are deep enough

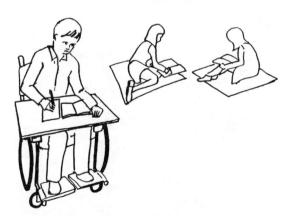

Portable work spaces provide comfortable ways to work.

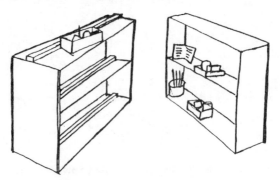

Arranging materials on the front of shelves keeps them accessible.

Materials can be accessible to different reaching abilities.

Large handles let children carry holders over a shoulder or arm.

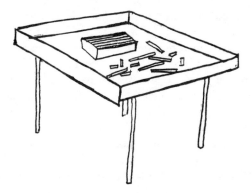

Work spaces with raised edges prevent spilling.

so as not to spill. Work spaces with raised edges allow for knocking over materials or spilling parts out of containers; pieces don't end up on the floor. Wherever pencils, pens, or other recording tools are located, providing large marking pens, giant crayons, and pencils in special holders lets children with grasp problems record on paper.

Reducing Visual and Auditory Stimuli

With a combination of materials arrangement and spatial organization, teachers can organize the environment to support children who need to work in settings with controlled visual or auditory stimuli. Perceptually clear display of materials on shelves, and careful placement of storage furniture to reduce the amount of visual information present in any one area, help reduce the level of stimulus. Spatial arrangements that

Large-sized recording tools help children with grasp problems.

create insulated and partially screened units are also helpful, as they provide shelter for the child trying to focus attention. These sheltered units limit the visual information each child must deal with inside the unit. When sound must be controlled to meet children's needs, there are some fairly simple ways to use materials that absorb or muffle extraneous noises. Spatial arrangement to shelter individuals and small groups from intrusion also helps separate the sounds of different areas.

Patterned backgrounds on walls, windows, furniture, and display facilities confuse the visual information of learning materials and work displays. Large, unpatterned place mats on shelves, on the other hand, offer a focusing background for somewhat smaller holders and organizers. Within the holders, different materials can also be separated to increase visual clarity.

Small shelving units, with a few materials on each shelf, offer less visual distraction than larger shelf units with many materials. Turning the shelf units so that most materials are not visible from outside the areas also cuts down the visual stimuli. Partially screened units offer shelter from visual and auditory stimuli, especially when sound-absorbing furniture and carpeting are used to define the spaces. Fabric on dividers and carpet on shelf surfaces also help reduce noise that can confuse

Patterned backgrounds confuse visual information.

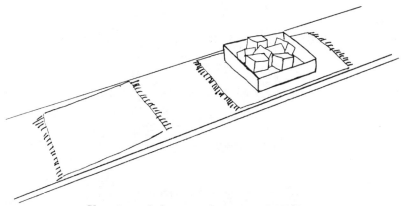

Unpatterned place mats focus material holders.

children who have difficulty sorting out auditory stimuli. Similarly, carpet samples placed on desks, tables, or cabinet tops can receive small, hard objects like puzzle pieces or button collections with a minimum of distracting sound.

Offering Maximum Visual Information

There may be children in a group who need a great deal of visual information in the environment because of hearing difficulties or language problems. Arranging and distributing materials to offer clear and consistent information about procedures helps such children negotiate the school day comfortably. Responsibilities for care of materials can be

Materials offer less visual distraction when they are visible inside, but not outside, the units.

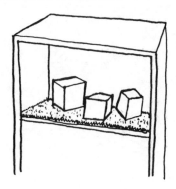

Carpet on shelf surfaces reduces noise.

communicated by including the equipment to do this with the materials themselves. Children can be shown how and where to return materials after use through holders and shelf arrangements that facilitate this.

The material arrangements that create a perceptually clear environment can also produce considerable visual information for children. Clear display of sets of material in holders, with different parts of the set shown in their own small organizers, can suggest relationships among the parts and possibilities for using them together. Display that highlights the attributes of materials makes it easier to notice the materials and to understand possibilities for their use in learning activities.

Spatial organization also offers visual information in the form of behavioral invitations. Long, straight paths running the length of the environment and large, empty spaces in the center of things invite different behaviors than short, diagonal paths through the environment with interesting things to see along the way.

Small, hard objects are quieter on carpeting.

Children who depend on visual information can be helped to meet teacher expectations, when the visual information of material arrangements and space reflects teachers' planned procedures and conveys the kinds of learning activities that are appropriate. The information offered by the environment's materials and space can be extended through opportunities to observe other children operating in the environment within those teacher expectations.

Perceptually clear display focuses visual information and reduces visual distraction. This is achieved by arranging materials within plain, large holders, and by leaving empty space around each holder. Spatial organization that creates paths which turn corners gives a visual suggestion for unhurried movement. When materials are arranged alongside the paths, scanning or browsing through materials is suggested.

Felt or soft pads can be included in holders containing fragile learning materials to be spread out. Such arrangements indicate how to care for the materials while in use and indicate that they are fragile. Sometimes games can be arranged with a sample showing how parts are combined; the visual information helps children understand how the materials are used. When materials that can be used together are grouped in a single holder, they offer visual information through their display. Choice is offered by providing a variety of tools that can be used on any raw material.

Arranging for Limited Vision

Spatial arrangement—especially the choice of furnishings to define space boundaries—and careful materials arrangement can help children with limited vision negotiate the environment and locate materials.

Visual information is focused by plain holders and empty space.

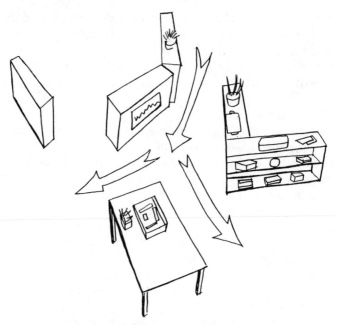

Paths can give visual suggestions for unhurried movement.

When space is divided by cabinets, bookcases, or screens that are waist high or taller, they are easier to perceive than subtler divisions such as carpet edges or color changes. The physical presence of space-defining furniture also helps children negotiate space through contact, if seeing is difficult. Arranging work places for pairs or small groups of children

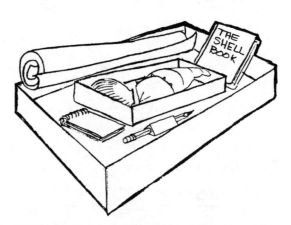

Including felt with fragile materials shows how to care for materials during use.

A sample shows how game parts are combined.

encourages sharing of competencies and knowledge in learning activities, with the skills of one child complementing those of another.

Careful display of materials helps everyone locate and replace materials, and at the same time promotes consistent placement of each group of provisions in its own place. Then materials can easily be found by children both with and without vision problems. The use of appro-

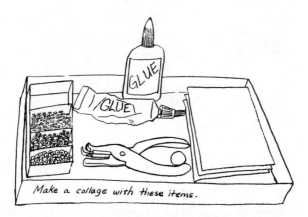

Grouping materials to be used together offers visual information.

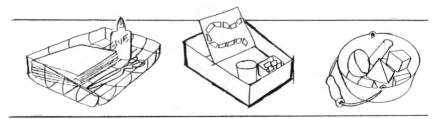

Size, shape, and texture differences help tell holders apart.

priate carriers for materials can prevent spilling of hard-to-find small pieces, and make it easier for everyone to gather sets of materials together before returning them to the shelves.

The environment's provisions can also support learning experiences of children with limited vision and help them work within the framework of their strengths. Including tools, raw materials, and information sources that don't require extensive vision in arrangements with others that demand it, can let the partially sighted child participate with other children in their learning activities.

Size, shape, and texture differences among holders and organizers make it easier for children to know which is which, even when vision is limited. Materials that can be handled and manipulated can be combined with information sources that don't demand extensive vision. In this way complexity is arranged in the materials groupings, and several choices for activity are offered children with vision problems.

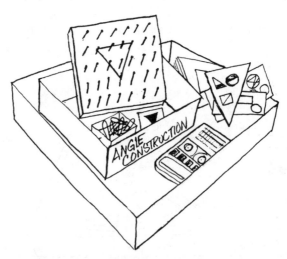

Complexity can be provided in material combinations that don't require normal vision.

Sheltered work spaces encourage the sharing of skills and information.

Spatial organization emphasizing cooperative settings for work encourages the spontaneous sharing of skills and information among children of different competencies. Sheltered work spaces for two or three, and partially screened units for three or four, can meet the needs of both partially and fully sighted children.

Meeting Varied Achievement Levels

Provisioning offers an immediate way for teachers to meet the range of achievement levels present in any group of learners. When exceptional children who are in some way handicapped or gifted join a group, close attention to provisioning is especially important. In their more direct instructional sessions with children, teachers use materials that meet each individual's level of academic functioning and encourage extension of those abilities. In a somewhat different way, the environment can meet the levels of many individuals at the same time, and encourage further growth by providing enough variety in basic provisioning so that all children encounter learning materials usable at their current levels of functioning and materials that help them reach further. The stimulation for growth comes from the opportunities to try out new skills; from invitations to explore new knowledge; and from being able to take advantage of peer help, or observe and join children using materials in different ways or at more advanced levels.

Diversity in provisioning offers tools and materials that can be used in simple or sophisticated ways; information sources that yield data with and without literacy skills; and information on a variety of subjects and topics ranging from those close to the concrete daily experiences of children to more abstract and complex ideas. Provisioning with variety provides frequent practice for children who are just beginning to develop

Information sources for different levels allow children to work together.

skills, while offering choice to those whose skills are highly developed. Variety in the basic provisions can offer vocabulary growth and enrichment for children at all levels of development, while stimulating thinking processes and conceptual development.

A collection of information sources that can be used on very different levels gives children of varied achievement a way to participate in learning activities together. Tools and materials can offer similar processes, but at different levels of sophistication, to meet the needs of many different children. When provisions for composing stories support children who must dictate their stories and those who can write their own first and second drafts, everybody has access to the experience.

Checking Your Own Environment

You can examine your environment for potential barriers and support for special children by looking closely at spatial arrangement, provisioning variation, and materials arrangement in terms of a general group of special needs. This can be done without children in the environment, but you will want to verify your findings by observing children with special needs as they attempt to gain access to the spaces, materials, and activity possibilities offered to their classmates.

Provisions can offer similar processes at different levels of sophistication.

Most teachers prefer to check one part of the environment at a time. When there are many developed and provisioned spaces within the environment, it is useful to assess each unit separately. In some environments the checklist can be applied to larger areas, with four to six geographical zones examined at one time.

1. Set up a checklist (similar to the one on page 230) to record your findings in each area examined, using the lists below. For each item on the checklist, indicate whether this arrangement is absent, present, or very strongly represented.
2. Covering one area at a time, examine the space, provisioning, and materials arrangement. Look for the following:

SPATIAL ARRANGEMENT

Space
— Paths wide enough for negotiation by wheelchair, crutches
— Areas large enough to accommodate movement with chair, crutches
— Space divisions offer visual shelter
— Space divisions offer noise shelter

Work Spaces
— Work spaces at varied levels
— Work spaces of different types

PROVISIONING

Information Sources
— Different content areas represented
— Different content levels represented

	AREAS	LARGE GROUP AREA	AREA NEAR PIANO
SPACE			
PATHS - WIDE		Strong	
LARGE AREA			
VISUAL SHELTER			PRESENT
NOISE SHELTER		Absent	
WORK SPACE			
VARIED LEVELS		PRESENT	ABSENT
Different types		STRONG	Absent
INFORMATION SOURCES			
Different content areas			
Different levels			
Visual & Non-Visual			
Print & Non Print			
RAW MATERIAL			
Diff. Manual Skills			
Diff Sense Stim.			
Tools			
Diff Skill Levels			
Diff phys. Abilities			
Materials Arrangement			

A checklist for arrangements to support special needs.

— Visual and nonvisual
— Print and nonprint

Raw Materials
— Require different manual skills
— Vary in sense stimulation

Tools
— Call upon different levels of skill
— Require different physical abilities

MATERIALS ARRANGEMENT

Stimulus Control
— Uncrowded, materials focused
— Arrangements to reduce noise
— Materials visible in areas, but not outside

Consistent Placement
— Materials gathered in holders
— No stacking
— Spacing between material groups

Holders and Organizers
— Vary in texture, shape, appearance
— Handles for carrying
— Designed to reduce spilling
— Display of materials suggests connections

Location
— Similar materials shelved at different heights
— Assortments of provisioning categories in each area

As you look over your findings on the record sheet, notice areas of the environment that show many arrangements missing. Those areas probably contain more barriers than supports for children with special needs. As you look at the record across each arrangement row, you can predict where special children will find barriers—within those arrangements with many negative entries.

It's not difficult to begin removing barriers and providing support for special needs by reorganizing parts of the environment where you have found potential problems. Observations of specific children will show what additional arrangements will strengthen the environment's support for all the children who work in it.

APPENDIX

Environmental Problem Solving

Environmental analysis is a useful tool for understanding puzzling behaviors and classroom events that distract from teaching and learning. An examination of the physical environment will often suggest changes of space, materials, or provisioning that can improve the situation.

Several common teacher-identified classroom problems, with related environmental arrangements, are listed in this appendix. For each problem, possible environmental causes are cited to guide teachers in analyzing their own environments. Chapters with further information about each environmental arrangement are identified.

Children often complain about one another's behavior.

Look for the presence of:	See Chapter
paths intersecting the surrounding space of work spaces	3
centralized storage of materials	7
dead space	3
overlapping surrounding space	3
potential units unrecognized by staff	3

Children need help in finding things to do and locating provisions.

Look for the presence of:	See Chapter
predominantly simple units and materials	5,7
materials displayed above children's eye level	2,6

materials in closed storage	5,6
stacked materials	6
crowded storage shelves	6
camouflaged materials in decorated holders	6
centralized storage of materials	7
materials stored beyond children's reach	6,9
work spaces and material storage separated	2,7
visual barriers at children's eye level	2,3,6

Look for the absence of:

face-out display	6
variety in provisioning	5
visually clear shelf display	6
material display to clarify use	6
holders that highlight materials	6
all provisioning categories represented	5
complexity in material groupings	7
empty space between materials on shelves	6
holders to facilitate carrying	6
complexity	5,7
variety of work spaces	2,5,9
common tools and materials in every area	3,7,8,9
clear paths through the environment	3,9
screened or sheltered work spaces	2,3,4,9

Children don't settle down or stay involved without teacher direction.

Look for the presence of:	See Chapter
overlapping surrounding space	3
paths through surrounding space	3
materials stored away from work spaces	2,7
traffic pattern through dead space	3
materials stored above children's eye level	2,6
predominantly simple materials	5,7
all work spaces grouped together	2

Look for the absence of:

work spaces for individuals or small groups	2,3,9
materials near work spaces	7
screened or sheltered work spaces	2,3,4,9
complexity in units or materials	5,7
material display to clarify use	6
materials stored within children's reach	6,9

Most classroom interest centers aren't used after the first few days.

Look for the presence of:	See Chapter
predominantly simple units and materials	5,7
small, crowded work spaces	2,3,4
overlapping surrounding space	3
Look for the absence of:	
paths leading to centers	3
work space within the center	2,4,5
complexity of materials	7
tools, materials, information sources together	3,8
variety of provisioning within centers	5,8
partial screening of centers	3,8,9

Paper, markers, masking tape, and so forth, disappear from shelves.

Look for the presence of:	See Chapter
centralized storage of materials	7
crowded shelves	6
materials in closed storage	6
materials stored away from work spaces	2,7
Look for the absence of:	
visually clear materials display	6
common tools and materials in every area	7
holders selected to highlight materials	6
materials near work spaces	2,7,8
variety of tools for common needs	5,7,8

During work session there is a lot of noise and random movement.

Look for the presence of:	See Chapter
centralized storage of commonly used tools	2,7
paths intruding into surrounding space	3
simple materials and material groupings	5,7
centralized storage of information sources	4,7,8
overlapping surrounding space	3
dead space	3

Look for the absence of:

complexity in materials	5,7
collections of common materials in every area	5,7
variety of clearly designated work spaces	2,3,4,5
perceptual clarity in material arrangement	6,9
partially screened activity units	3
clear and empty paths	3

The same children need redirection every day and never finish anything.

Look for the presence of:	See Chapter
overlapping surrounding space at work locations	2,3
paths intruding into surrounding space	2,3
centralized storage of materials	7
materials stored away from work spaces	2,7
all work spaces grouped together	2
Look for the absence of:	
complexity in areas where the children work	5,7
space divisions between work spaces and paths	3
all spaces of the environment available for child use	2
materials and space reflecting children's community	2,5

Most of the children show very short attention spans.

Look for the presence of:	See Chapter
overlapping surrounding space	3
predominantly simple materials	5,7
paths intruding into surrounding space	3
crowded material display	6
centralized material storage	9
all work spaces grouped together	2
Look for the absence of:	
variety in provisions	4,5
common tools and materials in every area	5,7,8
containers to encourage project continuation	4,5

several different kinds of work spaces	3,4,5
complexity in material groupings	7
materials display that clarifies use	6
work spaces large enough for children and their materials	5
material storage within children's reach	6,9

Pieces of games and puzzles are lost, broken, or misplaced.

Look for the presence of:	See Chapter
centralized storage of small equipment	7
crowded shelves	6
materials still in commercial boxes	6
materials that look alike	6
stacked materials	6
materials in closed boxes	6
small holders filled to the brim	6
holders that look alike	6
Look for the absence of:	
holders designed as carriers	6
large holders	6
holders that highlight differences between materials	6
decentralized storage of games and puzzles	6,7

One well-arranged activity unit is hardly ever used.

Look for the presence of:	See Chapter
unit located at far end of a path passing high-interest units	3
visual barriers concealing path from children's eye level	3
path intersecting surrounding space of another unit	3
furniture hiding materials in unit	3,6
predominantly simple materials in the unit	5,7
Look for the absence of:	
clear path leading to unit	3
complexity of materials in the unit	4,7

    materials reflecting children's community   5

    space reflecting children's community   2

Certain areas develop a commotion at the end of an activity period.

Look for the presence of:	See Chapter
several storage units located in the same area	2,7
centralized material storage	7
single location for turning in materials	7
centralized storage of cleanup equipment	7
dead space	3
main paths to storage units that enter surrounding spaces	3
Look for the absence of:	
several different locations for much-used material	2,7
multiple locations for material pickup and return	7
clear path to storage areas	3
decentralized personal storage	2,7

Children are using the learning materials "all wrong."

Look for the presence of:	See Chapter
materials intended for separate use displayed together	3,7
predominantly simple materials and activity units	5,7
overlapping surrounding space that puts materials together	3
Look for the absence of:	
material display to clarify use	6
display focus on significant attributes of materials	6
complexity in activity units	5,7
raw materials, tools, containers, and information sources identified through location and display	4,5
provisioning that includes all basic categories	4,5
materials reflecting children's community	5

Some of the materials in a popular area of the environment are seldom used.

Look for the presence of:	See Chapter
closed storage boxes	6
patterned storage boxes camouflaging materials	6
stacked materials	6
overstuffed storage shelves	6
simple materials	5,7
equipment in need of repair	4,5
Look for the absence of:	
tools and materials combined to increase possibilities	7,8,9
open holders and organizers	6
empty spaces between materials on shelves	6
visual clarity and focus in materials arrangement	6
complexity	5,7
related materials grouped nearby	7,8

Many children choose the same materials over and over again.

Look for the presence of:	See Chapter
materials in closed containers	6
small proportion of complex materials	5,7
many materials stored in closed cabinets	6
materials hidden on crowded shelves	6
paths beginning beside high-interest units	3,7
unused materials beyond children's reach	6
used materials familiar in children's community	5
centralized storage of materials	7
Look for the absence of:	
provisioning that includes all basic categories	4,5
decentralized distribution of materials	7
complexity	5,7
collection of common tools and materials in all areas	5,7,8,9

Nothing is ever where anybody can find it.

Look for the presence of: See Chapter
   centralized material distribution   7
   closed holders for materials   6
   stacked materials on crowded shelves   6
   separation of work spaces and materials   2,7
   decorated holders and organizers   6
   holders and organizers that look alike   6
   materials stored above children's eye level   6
Look for the absence of:
   visual clarity in materials arrangement   6,9
   widespread distribution of materials and tools   7
   empty spaces for materials return   6,9
   consistency of material placement   6,9
   holders to highlight materials   6
   spillproof holders and organizers   6,9
   materials shelved within children's reach   6,9
   marked areas on shelves for materials
      placement   6,9

BIBLIOGRAPHY

Atkinson, Bryan R., and Seunath, Oswald H. "The Effect of Stimulus Change in Attending Behavior in Normal Children and Children with Learning Disorders." *Journal of Learning Disabilities* 6 (1973): 569–73.

Bagford, Lawrence W. "Site Selection: A Study in Futurism." In *Designing Learning Environments*. Edited by Phillip J. Sleeman and D. M. Rockwell. New York: Longman, 1981.

Barth, Roland. "On Selecting Materials for the Classroom." *Childhood Education* 47 (1971): 311–14.

Best, Gary A. *Individuals with Physical Disabilities: An Introduction for Educators*. St. Louis: C. V. Mosby, 1978.

Bigge, June, and O'Donnell, Patrick. *Teaching Individuals with Physical and Multiple Disabilities*. Columbus, Ohio: Charles E. Merrill, 1977.

Chomsky, Carol. "How Sister Got Into the Grog." *Early Years* 6 (1975): 36.

Coates, Gary J., ed. *Alternative Learning Environments*. Stroudsburg, Pa.: Dowden, Hutchinson, and Ross, 1974.

Cohen, Monroe D., ed. *Selecting Educational Equipment and Materials for School and Home*. Washington, D.C.: Association for Childhood Educational International, 1976.

Danoff, Judith; Breitbart, Vicki; and Barr, Elinor. *Open for Children, for Those Interested in Early Childhood Education*. New York: McGraw-Hill, 1977.

David, Thomas G., and Wright, Benjamin D., eds. *Learning Environments*. Chicago: University of Chicago Press, 1975.

Dean, Joan. *Room to Learn*. New York: Citation Press, 1972.

Dye, Joan C. "Relationship of 'Life-Space' to Human Aggression: Implications for the Teacher in Bilingual-Bicultural Education." In *The Bilingual Child*, edited by Antonio Simoes. New York: Academic Press, 1976.

Engel, Brenda S. *Arranging the Informal Classroom*. Newton, Mass.: Education Development Center, 1973.

Fraser, Barry J. "Assessment of Learning Environment in Elementary School Classrooms." *Elementary School Journal* 79 (May 1979): 297–300.

Gehrke, Nathalie J. "Rituals of the Hidden Curriculum." In *Children in Time and Space*, edited by Kaoru Yamamoto. New York: Teachers College Press, 1979.

Griffin, Peg. "How and When Does Reading Occur in the Classroom?" *Theory Into Practice* 16 (1977): 376–83.

Hall, Edward T. *The Hidden Dimension*. New York: Doubleday, 1966.

————. *The Silent Language*. Greenwich, Conn.: Fawcett Press, 1969.

Harms, Thelma. "Evaluating Settings for Learning." *Young Children* 25 (May 1970): 304–08.

I Do and I Understand. Nuffield Mathematics Project, vol. 1. New York: John Wiley & Sons, 1967.

Jones, Anthony S. "A New Breed of Learning Environment Consultants." In *Designing Learning Environments*. Edited by Phillip J. Sleeman and D. M. Rockwell. New York: Longman, 1981.

Jones, Elizabeth. *Dimensions of Teaching-Learning Environments: Handbook for Teachers*. Pasadena: Pacific Oaks College Bookstore, 1973.

Kritchevksy, Sybil; Prescott, Elizabeth; and Walling, Lee. *Planning Environments for Young Children: Physical Space*. 2nd ed. Washington, D.C.: National Association for the Education of Young Children, 1977.

Ledford, Bruce R. "Interior Design: Impact on Learning Achievement." In *Designing Learning Environments*. Edited by Phillip J. Sleeman and D. M. Rockwell. New York: Longman, 1981.

Loughlin, Catherine. "Arranging the Learning Environment." *Insights* 11 (1978): 2–5.

————. "Understanding the Learning Environment." *Elementary School Journal* 78 (1977): 124–30.

McKenzie, Moira, and Kernig, Wendla. *The Challenge of Informal Education, Extending Young Children's Learning in the Open Classroom*. London: Darton, Longman, and Todd, 1975.

Northcott, Winifred H., ed. *The Hearing Impaired Child in the Regular Classroom*. Washington, D.C.: Alexander Graham Bell Association for the Deaf, 1973.

Piechowiak, Ann B., and Cook, Myra B. *Complete Guide to the Elementary Learning Center*. West Nyack, N.Y.: Parker Publishing, 1976.

Povey, G., and Flyer, J. *Personalized Reading*. Encino, Calif.: International Center for Educational Development, 1972.

Probst, Robert. "Human Needs and Working Places." In *Learning Environments*, edited by Thomas G. David and Benjamin D. Wright. Chicago: University of Chicago Press, 1975.

Proshansky, Etta, and Wolfe, Maxine. "The Physical Setting and Open Education." In *Learning Environments*. Edited by Thomas G. David and Benjamin D. Wright. Chicago: University of Chicago Press, 1975.

Reed, Marilyn. "Reading in the Open Classroom." *Theory Into Practice* 16 (1977): 392–400.

Simoes, Antonio, ed. *The Bilingual Child.* New York: Academic Press, 1976.
Skutch, Margaret, and Hamlin, Wilfrid G. *To Start a School.* Boston and Toronto: Little, Brown, 1971.
Sleeman, Phillip J., and Rockwell, D.M., eds. *Designing Learning Environments.* New York: Longman, 1981.
Stant, Margaret A. *The Young Child, His Activities and Materials.* Englewood Cliffs, N.J.: Prentice-Hall, 1972.
Taylor, Anne P., and Vlastos, George. *School Zone: Learning Environments for Children.* New York: Van Nostrand Reinhold, 1975.
Taylor, Joy. *Organizing the Open Classroom, A Teachers' Guide to the Integrated Day.* New York: Schocken Books, 1972.
Thomas, John I. *Learning Centers, Opening Up the Classroom.* Boston: Holbrook Press, 1975.
Van Dongen, Richard. "Young Children Move Into Reading Supported by a Classroom Reading Environment." *Insights* 12 (1979): 1–5.
Walberg, Herbert J., ed. *Educational Environments and Effects: Evaluation, Policy, and Productivity.* Berkeley, Calif.: McCutchan Publishing Corporation, 1979.
Yamamoto, Kaoru, ed. *Children in Time and Space.* New York: Teachers College Press, 1979.
Yardley, Alice. *Structure in Early Learning.* New York: Citation Press, 1974.

INDEX